Leading Beyond the Ordinary
A Guide to Exceptional Sales Management

by
Joseph Livesay

authorHOUSE®

AuthorHouse™
1663 Liberty Drive, Suite 200
Bloomington, IN 47403
www.authorhouse.com
Phone: 1-800-839-8640

First published by AuthorHouse 3/18/2008

ISBN: 978-1-4343-3799-3 (sc)
ISBN: 978-1-4343-3800-6 (hc)

Library of Congress Control Number: 2008900760

Printed in the United States of America
Bloomington, Indiana

This book is printed on acid-free paper.

Dedication

To my wife Marie for her patience, support, and editorial advice—as with all of the best things in my life, without you this could not have happened.

To our children—thanks for helping to make my life a dream come true. I can only hope that you are half as proud of me as I am of each of you.

And to my mentors—thank you for your friendship, your wisdom, and your honesty.

Table of Contents

Preface

Reading a preface is a lot like browsing the menu of a busy restaurant before you commit to waiting for 45 minutes for a table—you want to make sure that the investment of your time and money will leave you satisfied. As a reader, you want to know what the author intends to say, and you want to know if it is going to be worth your time and effort to "listen." I appreciate that; it's what I do too.

* * *

Sales, as a career, can and should be an honorable profession. Since, however, that is not how the typical consumer would describe "sales," something extraordinary must be done for that honor to be restored—or established. I know that the only way for that to happen is for the sales team to be led by an exceptionally gifted and talented leader. But gifting and talent alone do not define a leader, it requires skill and insight as well: my purpose through this book is to address those—the skills and insights needed to successfully lead a sales team.

* * *

For my part, I have been in sales for over twenty years: about half of that time in personal production and the other half in some level of sales management. My entire sales career has been in financial services—giving me significant experience with the special challenges associated with intangible products. During this time I have been directly and dynamically involved in the growth and development of investment programs within the retail-banking environment. I have worked for and with banks, credit unions, savings and loans, insurance companies, and investment companies. I have been a teller, a banker, a registered representative, a broker, an agent, a sales manager, a regional manager, a national manager, a principal, a trainer, a wholesaler, and a consultant. By most measurements I have been successful; the various awards and plaques I have earned throughout my career, at least the ones that I keep, adorn a bookcase in my office.

Having recently launched my own sales and sales management consulting company, I am currently working with sales organizations from a variety of industries, both here and in Europe, to develop more effective ways to be successful. In the variety of environments, one thing stands out: effective sales and sales management are based in unchanging principles. The means of sales success in the United States is the same means of success in Britain; the principles of leadership that produce extraordinary results for a team selling tangible products are the same principles that work for those selling intangibles. My consulting work is based on these sales and leadership principles; principles that I have learned both by practice and by observation.

* * *

As a sales manager, trying my best to achieve exceptional results, I came to know the sense of responsibility that can, at times, nearly overwhelm. Early in my career, having been promoted to positions of leadership, I found that there was a lot more to being an effective leader than it appeared from the "outside." Being promoted to a sales managers role primarily because I was very good at selling was not bad, but it certainly wasn't enough. Like most sales managers, I had to learn the hard way— by experience and by example—how to lead. In that learning process I was privileged to have worked with sales managers who had done a great job teaching me what to do, and with sales managers who had done a great job of teaching me what not to do. I experienced the struggles that come with trying to build a successful sales team, against the odds and with no formal sales management or leadership training. I understand the frustrations of sales management and, yes, even the sense that sometimes it seems there is nowhere to turn for help—after all, when you are the "boss," the one with all the answers, how could *you* possibly need help?

I have been where you are and, with the help of peers and mentors, have discovered the way beyond the frustrations and struggles, to a place of confidence and effectiveness. It is the net result of all that I have learned along the way, from great leaders, great sales people, and great clients that I will share with you throughout the chapters of this book.

* * *

The truth is: there is a vital need for leaders in the sales environment; consumers and businesses alike recognize that fact. Leaders are made not born. Leading is a definable process, one that can be communicated and upon which improvement can be made. It is my goal, through this book, to communicate that process and its significance to you, to your organization, and—most importantly—to your customers and clients.

Introduction

What does it take to be a successful sales manager?

How can my team consistently exceed expectations and goals?

Can we earn and retain client loyalty?

How can we increase the quantity *and* quality of customer referrals?

Are exceptional results possible?

Which activities really make a difference for my sales team and how can I help my team do more of them?

How do I prevent unwanted turnover?

What can I do to attract and retain talented sales persons?

What tools do I have that will help me to develop competence and expertise in my team?

Is it possible to effectively motivate my team?

How do I get our money's worth out of sales contests?

When and how should training be used... or is training a waste of time and money?

What is leadership and is it really necessary?

These (and the other issues that I specifically and practicably address inside) are the questions that represent the greatest challenges for the sales managers with whom I have worked. They are also the challenges for which I, as a sales manager, was continually searching for help and insight. For those I know, too often, the search ended in frustration.

As a matter of fact, had I been able, in the course of my career, to find a ready-source of honest, real-world information to help me tackle these issues and be the best sales manager I could be I might not have been motivated to write this book. I still might not have thought it necessary if it hadn't become obvious that so many sales organizations had lost sight of the real value true leaders bring. Or, if, as a result of my research and experiences, it hadn't become more and more apparent that even for those who value leadership, there is a growing need for sharing the skills and knowledge required to effectually lead.

* * *

As to the value of an effective sales manager, a true leader: what I have learned both directly and indirectly has caused me to consider the sales manager role to be the catalyst for success in any sales organization. It is the sales manager that has the greatest potential to impact, influence, and inspire others. Great sales people are important, no doubt, but the fact remains that no matter how many people benefit from one great sales person, one great sales manager can benefit exponentially more people.

The sales manager has leverage: he or she can move, via influence, what brute force alone cannot budge. Sales managers make a tremendous difference for their sales teams either by enabling and equipping them to succeed—which inherently means that their teams have helped a significant number of clients and customers to succeed—or by failing to. If the typical sales person helps 100 people satisfy a need, want, or dream; the typical sales manager influences the fulfillment of 10 to 15 times that many dreams. But their impact is not limited to the sales team and their clients. Since companies cannot survive without selling their products and services, sales managers are in a position to affect the livelihoods of not only themselves and their teams but of everyone within the organizations for which the sales managers work.

As a leader, he or she can make the process of buying goods and services pleasant for the consumer, encouraging them to loyalty, and building the business's reputation. Businesses create products and services to solve needs consumers have; sales managers oversee the process of bringing the consumer together with those solutions in a way that is satisfying to both parties. When the job is done right, the impact of the sales manager's leadership results in an ever-widening upward spiral of success.

Along with the opportunity to influence and impact the lives of consumers, team members and the organization as a whole, sales managers must also provide inspiration and energy to their teams. The sheer volume of energy that a sales organization consumes, as they endeavor to identify and satisfy consumer's needs, is remarkable. Dealing with people requires significant amounts of positive energy, as does facing rejection: sales people must do both every, single day.

As consumers, we expect sales people to be sincerely positive and to be experts in their products, as well as in their ability to convince us of their products' benefits. These expectations make selling, even when it is done the right way, difficult and draining. This constant consumption of energy requires a sufficient reservoir from which to draw. Good sales people tend to have one of their own, but even the best find themselves tapped out at times: sales managers must provide a stable source of energy when and as needed. At the times when sales people are most devoid of their own ability to "press on," when they have encountered a serious "energy" crisis, a sales manager must be prepared to step in and provide new hope and motivation. A sales manager's willingness and capacity to be creative and innovative generate this energy... and that makes their role extremely valuable, and vitally important.

* * *

As for the need to clearly expound the knowledge and skills required for a sales manager to be an effective leader: the comments I hear, the studies I read, my own experience in the market place all tell me that there is a recognized lack of expertise being displayed by sales people. I believe this lack of expertise in the sales force can be traced directly to the lack of knowledge, skill, and expertise in those who lead. I also believe that most sales managers/leaders are on their own in their efforts to develop expertise, because the companies for which they work have not understood the need for effective leadership training.

To help prove my point I suggest taking a look at the resources available to help those who sell. Even at first glance, one thing becomes abundantly clear: a deficit in expertise among sales people is **not** due to a lack of information on the topic. There are numerous books, seminars, and training regimen for becoming successful as a sales person. Innumerable websites, endless tools, and a seemingly inexhaustible supply of methods, means and mindsets for achieving sales success can be found.

So many resources available, still the average consumer is not satisfied with the level of competency shown. Assuming that within the mass of information available *are* the keys to selling, the fact that there is so much dissatisfaction on the part of the consuming public becomes even more poignant. If knowledge is power, those who sell have a nuclear reactor at their disposal; yet those who buy suggest that the process is more comparable to the flicker of candlelight. How can this be? I believe the key lies with the sales managers and the leadership they can, but too often have not been equipped to provide.

In taking a deeper look at the larger arena of selling, what becomes obvious is that while those who sell are overwhelmed with resources, those who manage them are relatively ignored. A simple comparison to demonstrate the variance is found by searching the Internet for books on sales versus books on sales management. What the results show is that there is not only a nearly 30:1 ratio in volume, there is also a vast difference in style. While most of the sales books are experiential in nature, most of the sales management books are academic. Where sales people can draw from the experiences of those who have succeeded, sales managers are given theory. The difference doesn't stop with books either. This same kind of discrepancy exists when it comes to all of the other resources available to sales managers as compared to sales people.

Certainly there is a need for good sales people; consumers who buy from them have made that clear. I just can't help but wonder if a greater emphasis on the "coach" might not help the "athletes" perform better? Since there is a demand for good sales people then, it seems plain to me that there is an even greater need for good leaders to develop, coach and equip good sales people.

Actually, the reference to coaches and athletes is a perfect example of what I am trying to say. Athletes have tapped into something that has made a difference in their ability to perform—a principle of leadership in the form of coaching—and I am convinced this principle can and should be applied to our profession. But how can it be done? What does it take to lead others? And more to my point, what do you need to lead your sales team as they endeavor to effectively meet and exceed customer expectations?

* * *

Because sales management did not come naturally to me, in my desire to be successful I have had to analyze the sales management process: break it down into its definable parts and determine the most effective way to implement each step. Fortunately for me, the ability to analyze did come naturally. So, in the course of my career, as I have observed those with the proven ability to lead, I have not only identified specific actions that made a difference, but the reasons behind them—not only *what* worked, but *why* it worked as well. The same is true of my observations of and experiences with those who were not successful leaders: not only was it important to identify their actions but their motives too. Putting all of these observations and the resulting principles together has led me to write this book.

I have gathered insight and knowledge from just about every sales manager and leader I have known and laid them back out in the two sections of this book: the sales management process (Chapters Two through Nine) and the philosophy of a leader (Chapters Ten through Thirteen). The first section recognizes the leadership principles of sales management, breaks down the management process into its definable steps and provides you with not only my insights and experiences, but also those of hundreds of other sales professionals. The second section addresses the value and importance of your role as a sales manager, to your team, your company, and to the consumers you serve. Chapter One introduces the principles of leadership and lays a quick foundation for the ideas and concepts, terms and meanings that are throughout the remainder of the text and Chapter Fourteen summarizes my thoughts and intentions.

If you read Section One from start to finish, note that I sequenced the chapters to follow the steps of the sales management process, in the order they would occur if you had been asked to enter a new market and start a sales team from scratch. Though each chapter is designed to address issues of importance for an existing team, the book is organized in what I thought to be the most logical order from a "start-up" perspective. You may decide instead to read the chapters that address your most pressing needs or even to skip ahead to the end and read the chapters on the leader's philosophy. Whichever order is most helpful to you, is the right order to read it.

As you read, you will notice my decision to keep this as non-industry specific as possible. I have, on purpose, chosen terms and phrases that are generic. Occasionally, when I am trying to illustrate a point, I have referred to specific businesses and industries. Otherwise, my desire to be inclusive has meant staying somewhat general on certain topics—though not to the point of over-looking the principles you will need to be successful. To avoid lapsing into too much theory, I have threaded the story of a hypothetical business throughout the "practical" chapters. Since those chapters are organized to coincide with a business's development, the story begins with the company's founding and follows the growth of the sales team over a five-year period of success. This hypothetical example provides you with a non-industry-specific means of applying the leadership principles of sales management.

* * *

Businesses exist to identify and satisfy the legitimate needs of consumers through the provision of goods and services. Sales people are the conduit between the consumers' needs and their company's solutions. Sales—the effective identification and satisfaction of consumer needs—can and should be an honorable profession. For that to be the case, sales people must have demonstrable expertise in the sales process, as well as the many intangible or "soft" skills that are required when dealing with a variety of individual personalities. Being a good sales person is challenging; having the knowledge and skill needed to manage and lead those in sales is monumental. When the mandated operational and regulatory aspects of proper selling are included in the mix, the need for well-trained sales managers becomes quite apparent. Add to those the requisites for an effective leader—innovation, motivation, market analysis, human resource management, creativity, vision, and passion, and the exceptional value of an excellent sales manager is undeniable.

I want to be a part of restoring (or in some cases, establishing) the honor of sales as a profession—to do that I firmly believe that the role of the sales manager has to be recognized for its importance. I wrote this book to help inspire and equip sales managers to fill that role. I sincerely hope that your ability to lead and manage will be encouraged and strengthened as a result of what you find within these pages. I also hope that you will see your importance and value to your team, your company, and yes, even to the economy in general in a new light.

Thank you for allowing me this opportunity to be a part of your ongoing growth and development.

Joe Livesay, President
Consumer Driven Enterprise, Inc.
www.beconsumerdriven.com
jlivesay@mac.com

Leadership Principles for Sales Managers

- The purpose of Sales Management is to enable and facilitate the effective delivery of the company's products and services to a select market.

- The ability for each member of the sales team to succeed is dependent on the existence of favorable circumstances (the market's need for your company's solution) and sufficient resources (the adequate allocation of market potential).

- Finding the right person for the job is the most difficult task a Sales Manager must undertake: identifying, recruiting, hiring, and retaining sales persons with the knowledge and skills necessary to provide consumers with satisfaction.

- Goals set and expectations held must be based in reason; a Sales Manager must be able to clearly demonstrate his or her reasons for believing that there is ample opportunity for goals and expectations to be successfully accomplished.

- Effective communication is dependent on knowing and speaking to the perspective of each member of the team and in committing to attentively listening to what they say.

- In facilitating the team's success, a Sales Manager must believe in the team's value, assist them in overcoming the obstacles and challenges that arise during the sales process, and provide them with an environment that encourages innovation.

- A company's core values are clearly expressed through the path of least resistance created by the compensation packages, contests and sales campaigns it designs; how a company spends its resources is undeniable proof of its priorities.

- A Sales Manager is responsible to enable his or her team to develop expertise and to become the best they can; training, mentoring, and coaching are the primary means available to accomplish this development.

- There will be times when it is determined that a sales person is not the right person for the job; being motivated by the consumer's best interest will encourage a Sales Manager to handle those circumstances with professionalism and grace.

The purpose of Sales Management is to enable and facilitate the effective delivery of the company's products and services to a select market.

CHAPTER ONE

Leadership and Management

As a sales manager you are, in truth, being asked to fill two distinct roles; to oversee the sales processes and people *and* to be a role model and an example. In essence you are expected to manage and to lead.

Of the two roles, people seem to be more comfortable with that of management, at least as a title—the sales managers I know seldom refer to themselves as leaders. This may be the result, at least in part, of a desire to not overstate one's own importance—but that assumes that management is easier and less significant than leadership. In reality, when done right, both management and leadership are difficult roles to fill, each requiring their own unique skills, aptitudes, insights, and expertise. Anyone taking on leadership responsibilities is just that: a leader. And that includes you. But you are also, most likely, required to manage, and that is no small task either.

In the chapters ahead I will be spending time and attention on each of the *specific* skills and philosophies necessary for the exercise of effective sales management and sales leadership. For now, in the way of laying a proper foundation, I want to address the *general* concepts of leadership and management—concepts that can apply to anyone and everyone, no matter his or her career or function. To that end, allow me to begin with the principles of management, then examine the characteristics of leadership, and finish with a treatise on why and how the two can and should coordinate.

Management

Management, as a concept and as a title, tends to carry with it an almost negative connotation, representing the infamous "they" in most people's minds. You know the ones: "they said we had to file this report," "they want us to go to this meeting," "they don't know how hard it is to..." "They" are the ones who are always slowing down progress or instituting rules. For many, management is like balancing one's checkbook—a necessary evil... though rank and file employees are not all that convinced how necessary "they" are. This at least seems to describe the typical employee mindset toward management.

There are a lot of reasons why this view of management exists—some justified, some not. We need to leave this perception behind and focus instead on the vital importance of properly applying the true principles of management to the process of achieving the business objective. To do that, it helps if we are using the same meaning for the term, so I will give you my definition.

Management is handling or directing with a degree of skill; succeeding to accomplish; the judicious use of means to accomplish an end. Etymologically, "management" comes from the Latin word for "hand" and should therefore be considered in the context of hands-on, active involvement as opposed to a theoretical view or application. If we use this definition, management is not at all trivial, mundane or a hindrance to progress; management is instead a critical element to the successful accomplishment of any worthwhile endeavor.

Proper application of true management ideals therefore includes being hands-on, skillful, directive, judicious or wise in finding ways to accomplish an objective, and successful. When we are placed in a *position* where we have responsibility for helping our team or our company become or remain successful, we are *in* management; whether we are effective or not depends on how well we perform in that position.

Effective management is the result of the following: 1) finding opportunities to be directly involved in the process, 2) staying practical as opposed to theoretical, 3) recognizing the implications of cause and effect, thereby identifying which activities result in failure and which lead to success, 4) developing the skills and aptitudes necessary to help the team implement the business plan, and, most importantly, 5) actually *doing* all of these things on a consistent basis. In management, it is important to know what to do, vital to do it, critical to do it repeatedly!

Direct involvement
The goal is never to just manage, but to manage *effectively*. That goal requires insight into which actions, attitudes, and approaches will produce the desired outcomes for each of the team members *and* which will not. That insight comes from hands-on involvement with the team, *in* the process. Management must take place on-site, in the field, with the team.

A friend of mine works for a large technology hardware manufacturer and "manages" a team of customer service representatives in another country. I know teleconferences and web-conferences are quite useful, but true management, by definition, requires hands-on involvement. Though what my friend does may be helpful, even efficient, through no fault of his own it should not be considered true management.

Scientific theory, by definition, is the result of observation. Effective management is scientific in that it requires first-hand observation and direct involvement with those being managed.

Keeping it practical

I have a son who served in Iraq as an Army reservist. His original plan was to complete his college education, enrolling in the ROTC program his final two years of school, allowing him to fulfill his active commitment as an officer, having gained practical, frontline experience as a reservist. His motivation for this approach was that he did not want to be the kind of officer who came in with book knowledge and theory but without an understanding of what life in the trenches was really like.

Management should be willing to take the same tack. For example, if the team is required to make 50 phone calls a day, management must be willing to do the same—not every day, but on occasion, if for no other reason than to make certain that their management expectations are realistic. The purpose of doing so is not for management to prove that their phone skills are superior but to confirm that what is being asked of the team is sensible. Again, management is hands-on involvement with the team; experiencing on occasion what they are asked to do each day will keep it practical.

Cause and effect

The fact that specific actions produce predictable results is terrific news for anyone in management. That reality enables a manager to identify what needs to be done and how often it needs to be done to achieve a desired end.

Too often management is guilty of asking the team to repeatedly do certain activities with the hope that, somehow, a different end result will be realized. If, instead, the activities that are proven to produce the desired outcome can be identified and isolated, then managers can promote the repetitious execution of those activities and allow everyone to benefit from the resulting predictability in the outcome.

One of the primary functions of management is to do just that: identify and isolate the activities that produce success. Doing so allows managers to emphasize the "good" activities, encouraging the team to engage in them, while at the same time the "bad" activities (those that do not produce success) can be recognized and minimized, if not eliminated.

Skill development

While identifying desirable activities through a practical, hands-on involvement with the team, management gains in-depth knowledge of what skills and aptitudes are present and which need to be developed and enhanced in each team member. "Skill" is the ability to use one's knowledge effectively and readily, a learned power of doing something competently. "Aptitude" is an inherent capacity for learning, a natural ability. The administration of skills and aptitudes works on two levels: those currently present, in varying degrees, in each of the team members and those that can be and are imparted. Management, therefore, must not only have an inventory of the skills and aptitudes each team member possesses but also those the team members lack. From this inventory, management can design the necessary development programs, enabling the business plan to be successfully implemented.

Consistency

In the midst of the day-by-day challenges and changes of a typical sales organization, a manager must provide consistency. The business plan, the corporate objective, and the underlying principles of management must lend constancy to the need for ongoing growth and development in the team. Business is not static, and so course adjustments will need to be made. But that fact, whether as the result of obstacles encountered or just the natural turn of events, should not prevent managers from providing an environment of stability. Those in management must know how success is defined for his or her team, what steps are needed to attain that success, and how to help the team take those steps—over and over to get the same successful results!

Leadership

Management happens. *Effective* management requires focused, deliberate attention: in a word—leadership. The way I define leadership in this text is as follows: 1) clearly understanding the objective, 2) exemplifying appropriate behavior, 3) providing guidance and direction, and 4) effectively influencing others in the pursuit and accomplishment of the specified objective.

Knowing where you're going

Leaders understand the importance of the objective; they know that the destination determines the journey; they always start with the end in mind.

For business the objective is success: success as defined by satisfied consumers. Businesses *exist* to satisfy the legitimate needs of the consuming public. Businesses *succeed* by satisfying those needs more effectively than their competition. Business leaders also understand that as important as the objective is, it is never worth compromising principle in an attempt to achieve it. They know this because history is full of examples of companies that have seemingly found a short cut to success only to realize that the only short cuts consumers appreciate are the ones that provide *them* with appropriate benefits. And since it is the consuming public that ultimately determines which businesses succeed, their opinions matter!

Setting an example

Admittedly, this working definition assumes a moral assessment of what is deemed "appropriate" behavior. However, in any but the most academic and theoretic discussions, the necessity of such an assessment is unquestioned. It is expected that those in leadership will set the pace, will be at the front of the pack so to speak, when it comes to acceptable behavior. In the day-to-day realities of business, there are actions that are acceptable and appropriate toward fellow employees as well as toward prospects, customers, and clients: actions that result in the further satisfaction of an increasing number of consumers' needs. There are behaviors that encourage trust, confidence, and loyalty; conversely, there are behaviors that discourage those coveted responses. Leaders will do more of the former and less of the latter. Call it virtue, uprightness, professionalism, wisdom; it is the result of doing the right things at the right times, and leaders have it.

Along a similar line, where someone is going is much more important than how well he or she might get us there. I am not interested in being lead over a cliff, no matter how dynamic the journey. There are those who have a natural charisma who have led people to horrific ends. Though these "leaders" seem to possess the attributes of leadership, the inclusion of the "appropriate behavior" standard in my definition eliminates those individuals from the ranks of leadership. What they truly are, whether charlatan or despot, is beyond the scope of this book, but they are not leaders.

Not wanting to stray any further into a theoretical discussion, suffice it to say that leadership not only knows for what it stands, it can clearly express its justification for those convictions, and those convictions will result in the development of trust and loyalty between leaders and those whom they lead.

One last thought on setting an example as a leader. There is a very old story of an extremely wealthy man who was taking his family and wealth, represented by huge flocks of sheep, cattle, camels, and donkeys, back to his childhood home. About halfway there, his older brother, being excited to see him and eager to help him finish the journey so that his returning brother could see their ailing father, meets him and urges him to quicken the pace. The wealthy man's response to his brother's urgency has been an inspiration to me in my role as a leader in business (and as a father of young children). He encourages his brother to go on ahead and let their father know he is coming, but he must take his time, for he is *unwilling to drive his flocks or his family and do them harm*. Instead, he will lead them reasonably, ensuring that they all arrive safely and in good health. Leaders do just that: they *lead* and *exemplify* the right way to finish the journey, the way that ensures that everyone under their care finishes successfully; they do not drive those whom they are leading.

Vision

Once leaders have defined the objective and identified and exemplified those behaviors that more effectively lead to that objective, leaders must find a way to express that objective to those on the team. Though this may seem *more* important in the early stages of a business's life, it is just that kind of thinking that causes so many companies to stray off the path that made them successful.

Giving direction and guidance is not an event; it is an ongoing process that actually becomes more important as a business succeeds, not less.

It is too often assumed that those looking to leaders for direction will be satisfied with a single dose, an assumption that leads to confusion among those being led. The team cannot be inoculated with vision; leaders cannot assume that one "shot" will do it. In fact, that mindset defies the very reason leadership is needed! Leaders must "feed" the team on a steady diet of vision, direction, and perspective; leaders need to stay focused and committed to that provision. Since the horizon is always changing and the panorama always shifting, the need for perspective and direction constantly renews. No matter how well fed I was yesterday, I find myself hungry for another meal today.

Having vision is important; describing that vision initially and consistently may quite likely be the key to successful leadership. For the team, clearly communicated direction provides confidence in the vision with which the leaders are endowed and a sense of security that the employees are not wasting their valuable resources by doing what they only "think" they have been hired to do. They recognize their need for guidance and look to their leaders to provide it. Without it, employees can feel lost, insecure, and unsure of their value to the organization. With clearly communicated direction, they are released to focus on effectively, even innovatively doing their jobs.

There are times when sales people get off track, no longer making the progress they would like. If they knew how or where this had occurred, they would simply double back and return to the way that leads them to success; but they don't know. So they swallow their pride and ask their sales managers for help. It is at this critical moment that leaders must be prepared to give hope and clear direction to their team members. Leaders understand that clear direction comes from two underlying truths: first, knowing the goal so instinctively that changes in landscape and environment do not distract from the journey; and second, learning to effectively and consistently communicate the way to reach that goal.

Effective influence

Once the objective is known, the appropriate behaviors identified and exemplified, and the vision consistently shared, leaders still must get those for whom the leaders are responsible to join in on the pursuit. There are both general *and* specific aspects of leadership that affect the attempt to influence others. Determining the course of action and providing clear direction and perspective—concepts just addressed— are the somewhat general aspects of leadership. Knowing the members of the team well enough to be able to identify their specialized needs and learning how to communicate with each of them are the more specific aspects.

Taking the time to learn each person's individual "language" or way of thinking is one example of how leaders must apply themselves to the process of influencing. Due to the variety of backgrounds and experiences, we tend to have at least slightly different vocabularies from one another. And though our general reactions to a message will be similar, the little nuances, which often make the difference between successful and failed communication, are the result of our individual languages. If leaders are to be successful at influencing others, then leaders must know their team well enough to speak to them in a way that each individual member of the team can understand.

There are general things that every team member needs, and there are things that may be needed by any given member of the team: leaders will make provisions for both. By having a clearly defined objective and the strategies to accomplish that objective, leaders have influence. Knowing the specific traits, characteristics, strengths, and needs of each member of the team enables that influence to be effective. This is part of what makes true leadership such a challenging venture and what makes it so rare.

Leadership AND Management

Now that we have examined the individual aspects of the two essential parts of what is typically expected from you as a sales manager, assistant vice-president of sales, mucky-muck of marketing, or whatever other title you may have been given, the question remains: "how do the principles of management and leadership interact?" And the equally important question: "can I do both?"

The information you have just read should have given you hope regarding your ability to fill both roles successfully, but to release your confidence completely, allow me to hone the point.

Both leadership and management suggest ground-level involvement, direct knowledge of the "who" and the "what"—the team and the process—but they also benefit from knowing the "why." Leadership demonstrates and communicates that which management identifies and imparts. Management *knows*; leadership *shows*. Management *gives* out principles of success; leadership *lives* out those principles. Management focuses on setting the course and ensures that the team is equipped and prepared; leadership focuses on successfully traveling the course and enabling the team to reach the goal—both are dynamic and responsive.

As a sales manager, your team needs both leadership and management and they are looking to you to provide them. For you to meet that need you will be required to re-think your role. It is essential that you believe in the importance of what you do, that you see yourself as a critical link in the chain of your company's success. It is not egotistical to recognize the value you bring to your team and to your company, it is simply an honest assessment.

Be the best manager you can by knowing your team, their needs, their strengths, and their weaknesses; be the best leader you can by demonstrating the skills and abilities as well as the attitudes and philosophies of excellence.

———×———

Leadership and management are congruent and complementary, but they are also unique.

In reality, most people who are responsible for determining or clarifying the objective, identifying the way of success to that objective, designing and communicating the business plan, and exemplifying its execution are not equally gifted in the unique skills and aptitudes needed for the two distinct roles of manager and leader. They have both jobs to do, but one typically comes more easily than the other.

If that describes you, you are not alone. But that is not to say that one individual (you) can't provide both leadership and management, because you can. You may have a natural leaning toward one role or the other, but since they work synergistically, you are well on your way to mastering both. Know your strengths and your challenges. Know what you can do naturally and what variances exist between your natural aptitudes and what you have been asked to do, and then develop the skills to bridge that gap. And, remember, you don't have to do it all on your own. There are others who, like you, are willing to pay the price of leadership. Seek out their friendship and allow them to help you get better in your areas of weakness, and then help them to do the same in return.

Section One
The Sales Management Process

Consumer Driven Sales Model

♦ Businesses Exist Solely to Satisfy the Legitimate Needs of Consumers

♦ Sales People are the Business's Most Valuable Resource: They are the Conduit Between the Consumer's Needs and the Company's Solutions

♦ Consumers Expect Expertise and Professionalism during the Sales Process Proportionate to the Resources They Expend

♦ Consumers Want Success for those Businesses that Effectively Satisfy their Needs

♦ Consumers Understand that Businesses Measure Success by Loyalty (repeat business) and Personal Referrals (new business) and are Willing to Give Both When They are Earned

The ability for each member of the sales team to succeed is dependent on the existence of favorable circumstances (the market's need for your company's solution) and sufficient resources (the adequate allocation of market potential).

CHAPTER TWO

Opportunity

Ours is a consumer-oriented economy. Consumers have needs, wants, dreams, and desires; businesses invent, design, and manufacture the means of satisfying those needs, wants, dreams, and desires. Consumers purchase goods and services, businesses employ individuals in the production and delivery of goods and services.

Consumers also have preferences and priorities. These preferences and priorities establish the basis for a company's success. It is not enough for a company to satisfy a need, want, dream, or desire—to be successful it must do so *better* than the competition, and *better* is defined by those being satisfied.

The process of delivering the goods and services that result in satisfied consumers is referred to as "sales." Sales management is the facilitation and enablement of the effective delivery of the means of consumer satisfaction.

The ability to successfully manage sales begins with a clear understanding of the depth and breadth of the *opportunity* that exists to effectively deliver consumer satisfaction within a select market. Are there enough people who want what we offer in the territory we want to offer it? Opportunity is defined as a combination of favorable circumstances or situations, the availability of sufficient resources to accomplish one's objective. For sales managers and their teams, the operative words are "favorable" and "sufficient."

Though somewhat subjective, the process of establishing the extent of existing opportunity suggests that by means of research and the resulting analysis, *reasons* to believe success is achievable have been identified.

Sales managers must use this kind of reasoned approach when determining if it makes sense to enter, support, or leave a specific market or territory. They must know if the circumstances are favorable; if success is possible. They must measure the sufficiency of the necessary resources. And they must be able to explain their decision—no matter the conclusion—with a demonstrable rationale.

The roles and responsibilities of a sales manager are many and varied and carry implications for their entire organization. Making the time and taking the effort to go through the process of knowing for certain that each member of the sales team has sufficient opportunity for success makes the rest of the sales manager's job significantly easier—not *easy* mind you, just *easier*. By being sure that the elements for success are available, a sales manager can drastically reduce the overall risk involved in his or her job.

The value of reason
The importance of a reasoned consideration of market opportunity when deciding to enter a new market, expand within an existing

market, or even replace an open position can be seen in at least two significant ways.

The first is in how this opportunity affects the lives of those who are recruited and hired to sell. Sales people are responsible to satisfactorily meet and exceed customer expectations; that depends as much on attitude as it does on technique. When a sales person is hired to match the consuming public's needs to the company's products and services, he or she must be confident that the decision made in accepting the job was a wise one. If there are doubts, they will be evident to the consumers with whom they meet. If the right people are to be successfully recruited, they must be presented with sufficient evidence that they will have the right opportunity.

The second way that this process shows its value is in how it affects the reputation a business earns as a provider of goods and services to the marketplace. Because of the repeat business and personal recommendations that result from it, a good reputation in the marketplace is synonymous with success. A good reputation, which is the consequence of consistently providing consumer satisfaction, must be carefully guarded. Though not easily earned, a good reputation can be very easily lost. The inherent challenge for any business to maintain its good reputation is that while there are several ways to do it wrong, there is only one way to do it right—and *right* changes based on consumers' preferences and priorities.

Inextricably linked to a company's reputation with customers and clients is its reputation as an employer. To provide clients with the expertise they demand, a company must *attract* and *retain* talented individuals. To attract and retain talent, the talented must *know* that they are valued, that what matters to them matters to their employer. If a company is going to treat employees as valuable, thereby gaining a good reputation as an employer, it must first thoroughly analyze the true market opportunity, making sure that whomever is hired will have favorable circumstances in which to work. Sales managers must thoroughly apply themselves to this process—the determination of opportunity—if the company wants to earn a good reputation, retain talented sales people and provide consumers with the expertise they desire.

(I understand that there are organizations where the only limit to the size of the sales force is the number of people who can be persuaded to go to work for them. Typically, these are high-volume, low-margin businesses. This model, which has no concern for reputation, might work when the product or service being purchased is relatively inexpensive and short-lived and when the primary driver of sales is convenience or impulse. It will always fail, however, when the product or service being provided has a relatively long life and requires a significant amount of the consumer's resources. The primary driver behind a consumer's decision to buy under those circumstances is confidence in the sales person's expertise in determining the best solution—expertise that requires experience, depth of knowledge, and exceptional skill. The content of this and the remaining chapters is targeted to those who are responsible for leading a sales team that is expected to provide expertise.)

Having reasons to believe that success is achievable, that both favorable circumstances and sufficient resources are available in your market as a whole as well as in each of the territories within your market, is critical to your ability to lead.

> You are a widget expert. You believe you have discovered a more effective way to satisfy the consumers' need for widgets and so you are considering whether or not to launch your own

business—Widget Enterprise. Knowing how many widgets the average household uses, how many households are in a given market, and how many competitors are vying for their share of widget consumption is only one-half of the formula for assessing your opportunity. The other half includes the costs associated with widget production, determining how difficult it will be to capture each percentage point of the widget buyers' loyal patronage, and discovering how much it will cost to acquire the sales person or persons with the necessary skill and expertise to satisfy those consumers. This analysis establishes the opportunity, or lack thereof, for your proposed business to introduce its solutions to a market.

* * *

The actual process a business might go through in measuring opportunity could be significantly more intricate than what was just described in my hypothetical model, but not necessarily so—it really depends on the complexity of the solution being provided. In any case, the purpose of this chapter is not to examine the sophistications of demographics and marketing but to focus instead on the importance of understanding the concepts involved in accurately determining opportunity. Those concepts include recognizing the company's primary objective, identifying an effective measurement or "proxy" of opportunity within the market in question, and determining the costs of attracting and retaining the right persons to provide customer satisfaction in that same market.

The objective

As I stated earlier, the objective of any company is success—effectively providing as much consumer satisfaction as possible is the means to that objective.

By exceeding consumer expectations and satisfying their needs, wants, dreams, and desires an organization can be assured of loyalty (repeat business) and personal recommendations (new business). There is a cause-and-effect relationship between providing satisfaction and achieving the corporate objective of success. For a business to proceed with confidence, it need only understand this relationship, establish the viability of the selected market, and obtain and develop those with the knowledge and skills needed to provide consumer satisfaction.

The proxy

The elements of identifying an effective measurement of opportunity include the following: knowing the demographics or profile of those who typically use the products and/or services that are being offered by you and your competitors, estimating the total number of "buying units" within the market who fit this profile, and assessing the share of those units realistically available to your sales team. As the sales manager, knowing the typical profile of your customers and clients should be basic. There are also numerous resources available through which to process those demographics and generate a reliable estimation of the total number of individuals who match that profile within a selected market or area. Leaving only the realistic assessment of your company's "share" of the potential market to be determined. It is here that the challenge is found; it is here that you demonstrate your leadership.

With time and experience, it may become possible (or at least tempting) to identify a single measurement that acts as a proxy of sufficient opportunity. If your business is established and if you are a successor sales manager, it is highly probable that just this kind of proxy has been used to determine opportunity in your market area. And though this approach can "simplify" the process, care must be taken to ensure that the measurement is and continues to be accurate.

In the bank investment program environment in which I spent a majority of my production career, a variety of measurements or "opportunity proxies" were used, some more effectively than others. The vastness of the range of effectiveness of these proxies provides evidence of the care that is needed when choosing such a measurement. For example, the proxy most widely used was pertinent and relevant in the early evolution of the industry (some twenty years ago). However, over time, the elements of the calculation have dramatically changed in response to market realities. A once valid proxy for opportunity in that industry, it no longer provides an accurate estimation of the available potential. It continues to be used out of habit, but has become ineffective, even detrimental to the process of determining true opportunity.

> As you analyze the merits of launching Widget Enterprise, you decide you want to simplify the ability to measure opportunity. In every market throughout your career in which you offered widgets, there was a recognizable correlation between the number of thingamabobs already owned and the number of widgets sold each year. This has caused you to consider using the marketing report for the number of thingamabobs as a leading indicator, and determining sales positions based on that report.
>
> Even though this may work more often than not, your closest advisors recommend caution on this approach. They remind you that even under the best of circumstances with the most consistent of results, marketing is never an exact science. They suggest that you should be willing to re-examine the process, at least annually. The fluidity of markets, the competitiveness of free enterprise,

and the variability of supply and demand warrant an analysis of true opportunity at least once a year, or more frequently if you are recruiting for additional widget sales talent.

The risks associated with using the wrong proxy or with miscalculating opportunity are two-fold. By *underestimating* the opportunity, your consumers are not satisfied because their needs are not met in a timely manner. Granted, in the short-term, achieving sales goals is not going to be an issue; the sales team is being inundated with favorable circumstance. Eventually, however, underestimation leads to an open invitation to increased competition and the loss of reputation and opportunity for your business. Consumers will only be so patient, and competitors are just waiting for an opportunity of their own to enter the market.

On the other hand, *overestimating* the opportunity means that the business will set goals and expectations based on faulty reasoning. Under those circumstances, even if there is a talented sales person in the position, he or she will not have sufficient resources to succeed, causing him or her either to leave for a better opportunity or to be let go because of a lack of productivity. This results in a waste of talent, the development of a bad reputation as an employer, and ultimately a lowering of the hiring standards—all of which lead to consumer dissatisfaction.

As a leader to your sales team, it is vital that you determine the "universe" of consumers who need the solutions your company and your competitors provide and the portion of that universe that is likely to utilize your solution. It is by effectively establishing and re-confirming the opportunity your team and each of its members has available to it that provides a foundation for ongoing success. Ease and simplicity should not replace accuracy in your efforts.

The cost

Finally, when it comes to determining the real opportunity in a market, it is vital to know not only the reasonable expectation for sales, but also the anticipated costs of capturing those sales. Those costs include not only financial resources but human resources as well. The business must be aware of its production as well as its distribution costs, taking both into account in measuring opportunity.

Fortunately, consumers understand that businesses need to make money and that a rewarding business relationship is bi-lateral. They understand that you need to make a profit; they just don't want you to make profitability your priority. Consumers are pragmatic; they know that for their future needs to be satisfied, good companies must be able to afford to stay in business.

There is an old story of a bakery that sold terrific bread for only a nickel a loaf. Their bread was not only better than any other bakery's in town it was less expensive too. The bread was so popular that every day people would line up around the block waiting to buy it as it came out of the oven. One bright morning, as the wonderful smell of freshly baked bread wafted through the neighborhood, the bakery's owner stood outside of his shop looking at the long line of anticipating customers. Instead of beaming with delight however, he was downcast and a lone tear rolled down one cheek. When asked why he was sad the owner gloomily replied, "Today is our last day in business." Shocked, the waiting patron declared, "How can that be, you are the most popular baker in the city; in several cities! You have people waiting every day for your bread, whose meals—whose very lives—will not be the same without your wonderful loaves—how can we convince you to keep baking?" The baker sadly looked him in the eye and bemoaned, "Yes, yes I am very popular and I dearly love all of my good friends who buy my bread. Unfortunately I am losing money on each loaf I sell and I don't seem to be able to make it up in volume."

The point of the story: no one wins when a good business closes, and consumers know it. If you are effectively satisfying the consumers' needs they not only want you to stay in business, they want you to thrive.

* * *

For their part, sales managers must know what it costs to recruit and hire the type of sales persons with whom consumers are satisfied. These costs will differ by market and will change as markets evolve. Though it is possible for a company to overestimate the costs of employing talented sales people, the more realistic risk is in underestimating it.

Underestimating the cost of attracting and retaining the right person for the job will result in providing less-than-adequate expertise to meet the consumer's demands. This will lead to a weakening reputation, dwindling sales, and eventually, even more turnover. Consumers want expertise during the sale; expertise is the specialized knowledge that comes only from either first-hand experience or mentoring. Turnover in sales people, which is the antithesis of developing expertise, can result if leaders are not fully aware of the process needed to determine opportunity and are not committed to paying the price of expertise.

The math

No matter the method or proxy used to determine opportunity, it will always come down to this basic formula: how much opportunity does it take for me to attract the right person for the job, how large of a territory or market area will be necessary to avail a good sales person of that opportunity, and is the hiring justified by the numbers. I have much to say about hiring and retaining the right person for the job in the next chapter. Assuming however, that I have every reason to believe that I have identified the right person, I do no one any favors by bringing someone onboard without sufficient opportunity. If I fail to effectively identify opportunity, I not only lose the benefits to the company that the right person would have brought, but I also erode my reputation as a good employer, making it more difficult for me to attract talented individuals down the road.

In all cases, the implications to the success of the business are serious enough to justify putting significant effort into the process.

Coaching opportunity

Before I leave the issue of opportunity, I need to skip ahead a bit and address how this issue can relate to the sales manager's role as a coach.

When a member of the sales team struggles to meet production goals, leaders cannot be certain of the source of his or her struggles unless it was determined from the beginning that his or her territory contained sufficient opportunity. If you were the one who hired the sales person and you assessed the opportunity prior to extending an offer to hire him or her, then you will know that a lack of opportunity is not the cause and can proceed to determine a course of action. If, on the other hand you inherited the team *or* if a current analysis of opportunity was not made prior to hiring him or her, you may need to re-examine the "foundations." If you recently inherited the team, it is even more important that you make every effort to analyze the true market opportunity to which the sales persons have been assigned, for it is likely that the original analysis was not complete—after all, you inherited the team for a reason.

Bottom line: there are always two sides to this equation. Perhaps the opportunity was misjudged, or perhaps the responsibility for under-performance rests on the sales person. As a leader, you must be *as* willing to reevaluate the assessment of true opportunity, as you are the effectiveness of any of your sales persons. An appropriate and effective measurement or proxy for opportunity should have been determined and applied *before* a position was filled. If not, you should take the time to assess it before a permanent human resource decision is made. Since the very nature of sales management is to be directly involved in observing and evaluating the skills and aptitudes of any sales person, discerning the reasons a sales person is not effective, be they territory or personal development related, should not be too difficult. Leaders must always make that assessment with open minds.

> For Widget Enterprise, assessing the favorability of market circumstances and hiring conditions means you need to know what the typical widget sales person in your market earns, the level of knowledge and skill that can be expected from an experienced widget seller, the level of knowledge and skill those who typically buy widgets expect, and whether or not your margins will allow you to recruit and hire that level of knowledge and skill or if you will have to hire at a level you can afford and then train, coach, and mentor your team to the expertise the market demands. Since you want to build your reputation as a great place for consumers to acquire widgets, you understand that you must also build your reputation as a great place to work, and so you must compensate accordingly.

To recap: the determination to recruit and hire a new member to the sales team must be founded on the business philosophy; when consumer satisfaction is the primary business motivation, recruiting and hiring expertise will be essential. Knowing the market dynamics for production and sales (supply and demand) allows managers to identify the true opportunity within a market. Further research on the cost of expertise allows sales managers to determine how much opportunity will be required in each territory; territories that will support the kind of sales persons who can provide customers and clients with a satisfying buying experience. The decision to build the sales team in this manner is supported by the business's philosophy that holds that the most valuable result of any interaction with the consuming public is to gain their trust, knowing that that will lead to ongoing growth of market share.

> For years you have dreamed of providing a better widget solution to your market; you have the vision and have gained the expertise to allow you to see that dream fulfilled. You have done the research: you know what it will cost you to make better widgets, who typically buys widgets, and how many widgets your market should buy in an average year. That research has helped you determine that your market should support the sale of 20,000 widgets per year and that your reputation and approach should allow you to capture at least 5% of that in the first year. The margins on widgets are such that the sale of 1,000 widgets will allow you to bring on two sales people with no real expertise or experience with widgets or one superbly trained widget guru—the most knowledgeable and skilled widget sales person in the market.

> Since your solution is centered on providing consumers with a satisfying widget buying experience, putting your resources into hiring someone who can facilitate that end makes sense. You are confident that by approaching widget sales in this manner you will continue to gain additional market share

through repeat widget business and personal recommendations from your satisfied clients at the 5% per year pace until you have captured between 40% and 45% of the total widget business in your area. This approach also gives you a solid foundation on which to build additional sales positions and the stability to retain your sales expert if it should take a little longer to capture the additional widget business. Based on your business objective, your understanding of the market opportunity, and the market costs of expertise in the widget business, you establish Widget Enterprise, endeavor to recruit and hire an expert widget sales person, and begin a long and rewarding career as the owner/sales manager of the most highly respected widget business in the country!

—◦◦—

Like every other responsibility of leadership, identifying true opportunity is done to create an environment where success is the norm. Success is defined by the satisfying of the legitimate needs of an increasing number of customers and clients. Satisfied consumers will reward their business partners with loyalty and personal referrals, leading to ongoing sales. This satisfaction depends on leaders knowing the real opportunity and designing territories accordingly; by doing so they give consumers what they want—sales persons who can be trusted to do what is the consumers' best interest.

Finding the right person for the job is the most difficult task a Sales Manager must undertake: identifying, recruiting, hiring, and retaining sales persons with the knowledge and skills necessary to provide consumers with satisfaction.

CHAPTER THREE
The Right Person for the Job

To be the best sales manager and leader you can, you must focus your efforts on enabling and facilitating your team's success. Those efforts require you to determine the existence of favorable circumstances and to divide your territories to ensure that each contains sufficient market potential. Once the opportunity has been defined and the territories designated, it is time to fill those territories with individuals who are adequately trained and equipped to satisfy the needs of the consumers in your market. Whether the open territory or territories represent existing positions or expansion into a new market, your most challenging responsibility just might be the identification of the right person for the job.

For most sales managers, building and maintaining a sales team with the ability to meet and exceed both the consumers' and the company's expectations is an almost overwhelming responsibility. The risks and dangers of recruiting can be intimidating. Attempting to identify in one or two hours, a sales person who is expected to be an effective part of your team for years can be exasperating. Too often the process has culminated with hiring a candidate who did an excellent job of talking the talk, but who later failed to walk the walk. Great interviewees who ended up being bad hires have frequently frustrated sales managers' efforts to build exceptional teams.

As difficult as this task is, there are certainly those who have proved themselves to be very effective at doing just that—finding that right person for the job that needs to be done.

What secrets do successful leaders use to identify these employees? How do sales managers who are effective as recruiters know what and who they are looking for? How have they solved the mystery that enables them to find, hire, and retain the right person?

The importance of recruiting, hiring, and retaining talented, qualified sales people makes understanding the answers to these questions essential for a sales manager.

Upon questioning those who are exceptionally skilled at recruiting and hiring, I have found their success to be based on the following common traits: having a clear, unshakable understanding of the *job* that needs to be done, possessing knowledge of the tangible and intangible *skills* needed to do the job, identifying the means to *measure* how and when the job is being done right, and having the ability to *interview* potential candidates in a way that pinpoints their qualifications.

(Leaders who have proved to be effective recruiters also have an understanding of what sales people want and need from leadership and a compensation system that allows them to attract the necessary candidates. The importance and nature of these last two items are such that they require a more thorough review, warranting dedicated chapters.)

Innovation

One sidebar before we examine these traits in detail—a sidebar that addresses a quality in talented sales people as well as in the vast majority of leaders, but that does not always present itself in the typical interview. This quality is innovation. Often in the recruiting process, a choice will come down to otherwise equally qualified candidates—for me, the deciding factor will be innovation.

By definition, innovation is the process of inventing or introducing a new way of doing things. Innovation is the willingness to risk "reinventing the wheel," not because you know that there is something wrong with the old wheel, but because you don't know that there isn't. Innovation says "why" and "what if . . . " when faced with a problem or challenge. Someone who has this characteristic has learned to think with the desired result in mind, examining each step of an existing process not with the intention to criticize but with an eye to improve.

Why is innovation important to your business? How vital is it that you, as a leader, welcome and encourage innovation? To illustrate the answers to those questions, let me draw from nature, specifically the characteristics of lakes.

I live fairly close to the Great Salt Lake. I have flown over it frequently and even toured it. There is no question that it is a lake—a body of water surrounded by land. I have been to many other lakes as well, to fish, swim, ski, boat, or just enjoy the scenery. Those, too, are unquestionably lakes. There is something unique about the Great Salt Lake in comparison to every other lake I have been to and it is not its size or the volume of water it contains. It is the fact that the water is "dead;" it does not sustain aquatic life. At seventy-five miles long and thirty-five miles wide, the Great Salt Lake is by far one of the biggest lakes I have seen, but it is also the deadest. Interestingly enough, it is not the lack of input that causes the Great Salt Lake's problem. It so happens that there are no significant outlets to purge the lake, to remove the impurities and make it vibrant. The other lakes I have visited have significant inflows *and* outflows of water; they are full of life because there is a constant flow of water. The inlets bring minerals in for the aquatic life to use; the outlets take the excess minerals out, together the flow keeps those lakes viable.

The parallels for a sales organization are striking: you not only need to recruit innovators and encourage innovation among your existing sales team, you need to give an outlet for that innovation—together a current of creativity is released. For a company, and especially for those organizations that are directly responsible for providing solutions to the consuming public, allowing and encouraging innovations does what the outflow of water does for a lake—innovations keep the company full of life. To carry through with the analogy, it isn't enough for your team members to bring new ideas and concepts into their roles. You must also give them the chance to let those ideas out, to present them as possible solutions that would benefit your clients. This constant flow brings and maintains life and balance. For a sales organization faced with the constant pressure to respond to the markets, innovation is the team's best hope for staying relevant.

At the same time, innovation need not be revolutionary to bring life; any re-invented wheel will still be round. I have participated in a number of "brain-storming" sessions where no option was off the table. After twenty, thirty, even sixty minutes of free-flowing ideas, the solutions presented are seldom revolutionary. Most often, the ideas that make the greatest impact are slight variations and minor deviations, not major overhauls (though that has happened on occasion), but they are "our" variations and deviations. Ownership and innovation make the difference; creativity brings life!

Innovation is vital for a sales team. So, how do you identify, within the limited time available for a typical interview, those with innovation? It helps to know its definition and value to be sure, but it also takes some insight and intuition on your part. In some ways, innovation is one of those "I'll know it when I see it" qualities. But it is possible to create scenarios that will bring it out, and doing that should be a part of your interview process. What has worked for me is developing a hypothetical scenario that expresses the challenges of the position being recruited, sharing the scenario with the candidates, and then listening to their responses—really listening, with the goal of hearing their *reasoning* for how they would resolve the challenges, not just *how* they would. The ability to know *why* a process is effective, not just the ability to reiterate a process, marks an innovator.

Again, many of the best recruiting sales managers I know are looking for innovators (some without even being conscious, until they find it, that that is the characteristic they are looking for). They may refer to innovation as an entrepreneurial attitude, a willingness to take risk, even an "I don't know what," but it is the very quality that most often separates their more successful recruits from the rest of the field.

> In your role as the sales manager of Widget Enterprise, you are faced with a decision regarding who will be brought on board to represent you to the consuming public. Your initial marketing research suggested that the opportunity could support either two relatively inexperienced widget sales people or one expert. Your business philosophy moves you in the direction of the strong foundation that would result from having an experienced expert as your first sales person. You know how to define success and, from your own experience in the industry, have a clear idea of what needs to be done to achieve success. You have placed

an ad in all of the widget trade journals and have begun to gather résumés and applications. You understand the critical importance of finding and hiring the right person for the job and believe you know the skills and aptitudes that that person would need to possess. You want to begin interviewing soon so that you can coordinate your widget production capacity to widget sales, but you are a little nervous about the possibility of being the victim of a "professional interviewer." In talking with your mentors, they recommend that you develop a pre-interview questionnaire that will allow you to obtain the data, the tangible facts you need, while developing a separate list of personal interview questions that will help you measure and compare the more intangible skills of the candidates. They also recommend that you keep your eyes open for an innovator, someone who not only knows what needs to be done, but why it is important to do it.

The *Job*

So, as a sales manager, you are responsible for enabling and facilitating the distribution of your company's products and services to the consumers in your assigned market. To accomplish this objective, you must have sales people who can successfully identify and satisfy the consumers' needs, acting as the conduit between the public and the company.

Those sales managers who have a demonstrated track record of finding that type of sales person understand that the first step in the recruitment process is *knowing* the ins and outs of the job. And though this may seem mundane, it lays the proper foundation for a successful hiring. They also understand that it is not enough to just know *about* the specific tasks and elements, but to *know* them, to be thoroughly familiar with them.

This is not to say that sales managers need to have been sales people, least of all top producers, for the skill set is vastly different. What I am saying is that the day-to-day activities must be understood and appreciated. This clarity and knowledge lead to an analytical assessment of the skills and aptitudes, tangible and intangible, which are needed for the sales person to be successful.

The knowledge of what needs doing is like the destination on a map. Without a well-defined job to do, there is really no way to effectively recruit. You must determine the destination before you can make progress toward the goal; you must see the target before you can take aim. You must know what the job requires before you can hope to identify someone to fill it, let alone help your team to do that job successfully. That said, one of the clearest dangers leaders face in defining the job to be done, and therefore in the recruiting process itself, is taking the short cut represented by *assuming* that the job description "on file" is the true, working job description. Though it may not be necessary or even possible to re-write the formal job description, leaders must seriously analyze its accuracy and alignment to the mission and then supplement it as needed during the recruitment process.

A true analysis of the job will require that you take the time to list all tasks and activities that you believe are important to doing the job successfully. Once compiled, prioritize them in two separate ways, by impact or importance *and* by time consumption (for we all know that there are very basic tasks that we are required to do that take up significant amounts of time). For example, when I was in sales production, returning a client's phone call was a high impact activity but one that typically did not consume a significant amount of time. On the other hand, completing the required reports had no direct impact on a client's satisfaction but amounted to about 10 – 15% of my week's time consumption.

After you have come up with your list and rankings, compare them to the official job description to determine if changes need to be made. I know you could just ignore this process, but there are times and circumstances that may arise that would dictate that these corrections be completed to avoid future costs and conflicts.

Next, take your lists and review them with your supervisor, your best sales people, and your peers or mentors to validate your assessments. Finding the right person for the job is perhaps your most important task. The ability to fulfill that task well starts with a thorough knowledge of the job the person will be asked to do, and getting valuable input from other experts to make sure you are well equipped to succeed is worth the effort.

The *Skills*

The natural progression of having a clear idea of the activities and tasks of the job to be done is the confident knowledge of the skills needed to do the job *right*. These skills will be tangible and intangible in nature. Tangible skills are those that are typically tied to measurable activities such as time management, marketing, needs assessment and analysis, communication skills (though some may argue about how measurable these are), competencies in industry and related product knowledge, and timeliness in properly completing any required paperwork. Intangible skills are those that are typically more subjective in nature, but equally important to the job, such as honesty, patience, confidence, "people" skills, and diligence.

As a hiring manager in the investment industry, the skills I looked for in those wanting to fill an investment advisor job would include competence in the areas of the products and services available, identifiable values and operating principles, recognition of how they themselves want to be treated as consumers, the ability to effectively communicate and an understanding of how important that is, acceptance of the importance of hard-work, and a willingness to take the necessary risks to bring innovation to the team. These skills were on top of the minimum licensing, education, and experience requirements that are standard for the industry. This list is by no means exhaustive, and I do not believe it is "better" than anyone else's in my same industry. Each person's leadership style and approach will have an impact on which skills the person seeks and the priorities the person places on them. But, when I stuck to this list, it was very effective.

Prioritizing the skills needed goes hand in hand with identifying them. In my experience, the subjective skills were always more important than the tangible skills, which by nature meant that the skills I considered most valuable were also more difficult to quantify. So having an unwavering idea of the skills needed in the people I should hire was critical!

Using your knowledge of the job that needs to be done and your analysis of those who are successful at doing it, create a list of the skills that you believe are essential. Categorize them by the means you would use to identify them in your candidates. The tangible skills are outward and measurable; the intangible are more inward and attitudinal—identified as much by *how* the recruit handles the interview as by what answers he or she actually gives. This list, along with the job description, will form the basis for the interview questions that you need to develop… but I am getting ahead of myself.

The *Measurement*

The best recruiting sales managers have a clear understanding of *who* and *what* they are looking for in the recruiting process. They realize that they must *know* the job to be done, the skills to do it, and the measurements to ensure the skills are being applied; then they need to develop an interview process based on their knowledge. The definition of the job and identification of those skills needed to do the job have been reviewed. Next, sales managers need to discover the means of measuring how and when the job is being done right. The first two steps were knowledge based, theoretical in nature; this third step begins the transition to application.

For example, if the job is providing investment advice and one of the skills needed for the job is the ability to accurately calculate the impact of inflation on the income that will be needed for retirement, then I am responsible as a leader to make sure that the tools necessary to measure compliance with the requirement are in place *and* to utilize those tools to confirm that the calculation is being done correctly.

This example uses a tangible process on purpose . . . by their nature tangible skills are easier to measure. Because of that, there has been an effort, in the realm of sales management, to try to quantify the intangible skills in much the same way as one would quantify the tangible. Usually this involves an attempt to simplify the sales process by measuring its most basic common activities. Though this can be a very helpful approach, it has its limitations and tends to lead to serious understatements of all that is actually required to get the job done right.

When I was part of the management team of a bank's investment division, we attempted to measure the skills needed to be a successful investment advisor by developing a spreadsheet that reduced the sales process down to a simple mathematical formula. This led us to the conclusion that a particular sales goal could be achieved if the sales person dialed the phone a certain number of times. We even went so far as to calculate the monetary value of each dial. Though this was technically accurate, like all technical analysis, it used the absolute predictability of hindsight while doing nothing to adjust for the future; the uncontrollable or unforeseen.

Taking this approach to its ultimate conclusion, the sales process tends to become mechanized, which is fine if we are selling to machines, but not so good when people are involved.

Admittedly, within certain statistical deviations, compliance with the identified activity measurements should result in attaining the desired sales goals. That fact, however, does not change the reality that this approach alone is like driving by the rearview mirror. You know exactly where you have been and have a reasonable chance of staying on track . . . as long as the road is straight, flat, and obstacle-free. The problem is—that kind of road does not exist. I am *not*, by the way, saying that leaders should not use this type of activity-based measurement tool as a way to gauge if the job is being done. (To carry on with the type, it is important to check your rearview mirrors frequently when driving.) I *am* saying that leaders must recognize the limitations of these activity-based measurements and be sure to make them only *one* of the evaluation tools.

Sales managers must also find an effective way to measure the application of the mostly intangible skills that make for superior sales people. Typically, this requires first-hand observation as well as feedback from clients, peers, and partners. Again, sales managers must *know* what it takes for a sales person to be successful in order for the observations to be helpful. They must use this knowledge to develop clear, concise forms and interviews that can be used with prospects and clients. This will take some time and effort, but the importance of these skills to the success of your team makes it worthwhile.

The minimum number of measurement tools I recommend is three, with a combination of quantitative and qualitative measurements. This will allow a leader to "pin-point" the sales person's position. As a sales manager I used two quantitative measurements based on key behaviors and a qualitative measurement based on consumer feedback. The qualitative measurement helped me differentiate between a job done efficiently (meaning with a minimal amount of effort) and a job done effectively (meaning with the greatest amount of impact). Once the information was gathered, it was my responsibility as a leader to use my knowledge of the essence and details of the job to interpret the results. Though the use of both qualitative and quantitative measurements required greater involvement on my part, it also provided a clearer gauge of the sales person's effectiveness and virtually eliminated the guesswork in evaluating if the job was being done *and* being done right.

These measurements and expectations become a very important part of the recruitment process in two ways. First, they provide a point of comparing a candidate's past performance with previous employers (assuming he or she is someone with experience) to the standards required for effectiveness on your team. Second, describing the measurement process to the candidate gives him or her a very clear glimpse of how you will manage him or her if he or she is hired.

The *Interview*

We have identified what the job to be done is, what skills (tangible and intangible) will be needed to do that job, and the process used to ensure that those skills are being applied effectively. The final piece brings all of this work together: how to actually identify the right person.

To recruit successfully, leaders must not only have sufficient knowledge in all of these elements, they must also develop an effective, yet sensitive, interview format that ensures that the potential employee actually has what the job requires. The more expertise needed to do the job, the more time that should be taken to formulate the "interview" and the more time that should be taken to assess a candidate's qualifications. When the job is complex enough, it is a good idea to develop a pre-interview questionnaire for each candidate to complete before his or her face-to-face meeting. This does a couple of valuable things. It demonstrates your commitment to the process and the worth you place on the job, and it provides you with a means of comparing one recruit to another, all the while allowing the personal interview to be just that—personal, intuitive, and responsive to each individual.

In much the same way as a consumer-driven sales model builds on the foundation of identifying the consumer's needs, a good interview is built on the foundation of identifying the candidate's skills—tangible and intangible. The questions you ask should be focused and deliberate while allowing plenty of input from the candidate. Since sales expertise is based as much, maybe even more, on intangible skills as on tangible, giving adequate opportunity for each candidate to demonstrate his or her true character is essential if those intangibles are to be revealed.

For Human Resource purposes, a scripted interview is probably going to be mandatory. Even if it isn't mandatory, it is a best practice that will provide you with a comprehensible means of comparison. Along with the question-and-answer portion of your interview, be sure to include a clear description of your expectations in all pertinent areas of the job *and* give the candidate the opportunity to express his or her understanding of the same. It is better for you (and him or her, for that matter) to know upfront if there is a lack of agreement on any of the vital aspects of the job.

Lastly, keep in mind that there are individuals who interview better than others, as well as individuals whom some have referred to as "professional" interviewers. A well-designed interview uncovers the candidate's real character and should help you avoid being "sold." You want to acquire a resource, so in a very real sense you are the "consumer" in this process. By approaching the interview in much the same manner as a good consumer approaches the satisfaction of his or her need, you will be better able to determine that a given candidate possesses the skills that will enable you to match your need to the most desirable solution. Admittedly, there is no perfect employee, just as there is no perfect job or perfect product; but that does not mean that there isn't a best employee and a best solution—don't settle for less.

> You have recently concluded your interviews for an expert widget sales person. In front of you are the résumés of the three best candidates. Each has plenty of experience in the industry, while two of them also have sales experience from other industries. They were all comfortable with the first year's compensation package and the opportunity in the market. They made it to the final selection process because they were all exceptionally skilled and gifted. Your interview process included a scenario that required them to explain how they would handle a client interview in which the client's needs could not be satisfied by your widgets. All of their responses demonstrated an understanding that the short-term loss of a sale would net the long-term benefit of trust.
>
> Knowing that as the business grows you will need to hire someone to replace yourself as sales manager, you also included a question that required each candidate to examine how he or

she would demonstrate leadership to those added to the team down the road. The response you received from one of the candidates has made clear to you who should be offered the position. Understanding the principles and value of leadership as an attitude, not just as the result of being given a title, has made Ms. Smidget your choice to be the first sales person ever hired by Widget Enterprise.

You move her application to the top of the pile and dial her cell phone number from your office phone—if by chance she turns you down, you will have to move to your second choice—one whom you could definitely be happy about but . . .

Ms. Smidget answers the phone; you make your offer, and she expresses her immediate and excited acceptance—she is thrilled to be a part of such a promising and positive opportunity. After some additional information exchange, you hang up, lean back, and revel in the knowledge that you have just hired the best person available to provide your customers and clients with a satisfying widget-buying experience!

One last point, and I leave it for last not because it is trivial but because it is so vitally important: selecting the right person for any job must be based only on matching the company's needs to the candidate's qualifications. As in every area of life, there is never room for any kind of discriminatory beliefs or practices in the hiring process.

You know your company's objectives, the skills required to do the job effectively, and the means to measure success, and you have developed an effective interview process that gives you a very good chance of identifying and attracting the right person for the job.

Even when done right, recruiting, screening, interviewing, assessing, and hiring are strenuous tasks—all the more reason for leaders to take their time to do it right so that it doesn't have to be done again.

Goals set and expectations held must be based in reason; a Sales Manager must be able to clearly demonstrate his or her reasons for believing that there is ample opportunity for goals and expectations to be successfully accomplished.

CHAPTER FOUR

Expectations and Goals

In my twenty-plus years of interaction with sales people, the topic of the complaints most frequently conveyed to me is the way their sales organizations typically set sales goals. It is not that they complain about having sales goals—sales people understand the value and importance of goals. It is that they are just not satisfied with how those goals are usually determined. From my conversations with them I have gathered that often, sales people do not believe that their knowledge, insight or opinions matter to those making the goal-setting decisions. This lack of inclusion makes them feel unimportant, even disrespected.

The lack of respect for their opinions may not, in fact, be real—but it is most certainly perceived. And this perception is reinforced by their experience: a decision of the magnitude of a sales goal is being made—a decision that will directly impact a sales person's life—and they are not given the opportunity to provide real input.

I have concluded that managers do not set out to be exclusive, they simply fail to grasp the positive impact inclusion will have on how effectively the goal will be accomplished. Not involving those directly affected by the goal-setting decision is often the result of a misunderstanding on the part of management, at some level, regarding how to set *good* goals or how to identify *appropriate* expectations. This misunderstanding leaves those setting the goals with an underlying, though often subconscious, lack of confidence in the goals' validity.

This challenge is magnified when a sales manager has spent time as a sales person (which is typical). He or she knows that those who are in direct contact with consumers have an innate insight into what is possible and what is probable when it comes to sales performance. If the sales manager is either not encouraged to seek input from the team, or if the system does not allow for that input, the leader knows that any goals set will lack an extremely valuable perspective.

It is also quite possible that the sales manager has had little input into his or her own sales goals—those that apply to the team as a whole. This reality can make it almost impossible for a sales manager to use a completely unbiased process in setting the individual goals that will apply to his or her team members. When this is the case, the only real choice a leader has is to be open and honest in communicating the process, allowing the opportunity for sales persons to at least benefit from the sense of "team" that including them creates.

Setting Good Goals

Based on experience, the description that follows may seem somewhat idyllic; however, to stay focused on those things that leaders *can* do to enable and facilitate success, I will address the most effective process for setting goals. As a first step, I will provide the opportunity for clear communication by addressing semantics. Since I have seen the terms "objective," "expectation," and "goal," and again "strategy" and "tactic" used almost interchangeably, here are the definitions that I will use.

- ◆ "Objective" is defined as the overriding purpose for which any business or endeavor exists.

- ◆ An "expectation" is a confident belief or strong hope that a particular event will happen, including a standard of conduct or level of performance. A "realistic expectation" then is an expectation that has a *demonstrable reason* for the confidence in the belief that it will be accomplished.

- ◆ The term "goal" is quite general in nature; it is defined simply as something that someone wants to achieve. The general nature of the definition means that good and bad goals can be set, as can short or long-term goals. I consider a "good goal" to be any desired achievement that will effectively assist in attaining the objective.

- ◆ A "strategy" is a carefully devised plan of action designed to achieve a goal, and more specifically a long-term goal or objective. This means that the effectiveness of the strategy is not dependent on the quality of the goal; a bad goal can be strategically achieved.

- ◆ Lastly, a "tactic" is a method used or course of action taken to achieve a short-term goal. I differentiate between strategies and tactics in much the same way as might be seen in military context: strategies are used to accomplish objectives (which are in essence overriding or long-term goals), and tactics are the actions taken to achieve goals.

Although other definitions have been and are used for any and all of these terms, these definition are those most widely held.

> For Widget Enterprise, the journey has begun: the objective has been codified in the corporate mission statement, the initial marketing research has been gathered, and it has been determined that a real opportunity exists to provide a "better widget experience" in your market. Every indication is that hiring the best widget sales person in the market will provide you with the most solid foundation. You have submitted your business plan to the commercial loan officer and been approved for the capital you need to begin manufacturing widgets. You know your objective and your goals, the strategies and the tactics you will implement to achieve them, and the means to measure your progress. You have recruited and made an offer to the best candidate you had found to become your first sales person, your offer was gladly accepted, and you have established Ms. Smidget's starting date. It is time to do one more analysis of current market conditions, confirm production capacity, and establish first-quarter and first-year expectations.

I firmly believe that sales managers desire the goals they set to be good—that is, they want their resources expended on those activities that will lead to continued success. A *good* goal, by definition, is founded on a combination of a clear understanding of the overriding objective and *realistic* expectations. Since we have already addressed the concept that businesses exist to satisfy the legitimate needs of the consumers in their select markets and acknowledged the importance of embracing that as the corporate objective, we can move on to recognizing the value of possessing realistic expectations when setting goals intended to aid in the achievement of that objective.

* * *

It is helpful to understand that a big part of what makes the determination of realistic expectations so uncertain is that "realistic" is, to some degree, a judgment call. Therefore, when considering the inclusion of input from the sales team, what leaders hold to be realistic may differ, sometimes dramatically, from what those "in the field" might consider realistic. This fact remains even though both parties use reason to justify their position. At this very juncture, a sales manager can have significant impact.

Let's say, for example, that you are responsible to set next year's sales goal. Currently, your best sales person sells 50 units/week and your average is 44 units/week per person for your entire sales team of 10 sales persons. Let's assume that you have been growing your share of the market by an average of 5% per year for the last five years and that your company currently captures 40% of the market. It would be reasonable, based on these facts, to expect an increase of 5 units/week per sales person for the next year—representing a 5% increase in market penetration over last year and utilizing the same calculation used in arriving at this year's goal. It would also be reasonable, since, as the company's market share increases, it will become incrementally more difficult to capture each point of increase, to expect an additional 2 units/week per sales person—a 5% increase over last year's weekly production. It might even be reasonable to expect a 6 unit/week per person increase based on an equivalent percentage increase from the prior year to this year (14.6%) being applied for next year.

If your sales team provided input, their reasoned conclusion could differ from yours by as much as a 200% variance. Since any of the listed goals could be justified, it becomes a matter of judgment as to which you choose. As the sales manager the final decision is yours. The key for you, since you have decided to get input from your team, is having a clear rationale to back the decision made and demonstrable reasons for believing that success is achievable.

This is a simple illustration that looks at only a couple of factors in attempting to determine a reasonable, realistic expectation—and yet, simple as it is, the complexity of the process is revealed. With as little information as was provided, three different goals were justifiable, and in reality, several more reasonable options could be calculated from the same data. As this example shows, it will require leadership, insight, and expertise not only to select the goal, but also to communicate it confidently. By including input from the sales team you stand to benefit from their insight as well as their willing help in achieving the goal.

* * *

The business model I am describing assumes that the company has chosen to establish itself on the principle that competition requires the company to serve the needs of its chosen market effectively—providing superior consumer satisfaction—and that that principle in no way conflicts with the need to use goal-setting in allocating resources. I am not suggesting that goal-setting is unnecessary or even that it is a necessary evil. To the contrary, proper goal-setting is necessary and good for the health and well-being of any sales organization. The question is simply one of process: who should be included in identifying the reasoned, realistic expectations upon which the goals will be set?

Ultimately, it rests upon leaders to set goals: using their knowledge of the markets, their understanding of the mission, and their insights into what it takes for their team to succeed. But "in the multitude of counsel there is wisdom"—wisdom being the repeated execution of those activities that produce the results desired. Seeking and attaining input from those who have first-hand knowledge of the market will only strengthen the case for the goals set.

Along with the insight that comes from the additional "intel" gathered from the sales team is a fringe benefit for the business: reinforcing a reputation as a great employer. Since the company's reputation is dramatically impacted by the retention and satisfaction of the sales team, including their input in the goal-setting process makes sense from a management perspective. I have yet to meet a sales team that did not want to be included in this process. By doing so, the leader demonstrates the value he or she places in the sales team, contributing to an improved sales environment.

There is only one risk leaders face: once the sales team has been included, any difference in the definition of "realistic" becomes open and apparent. However, even when there is a difference, including the team's input is still a good policy. Since the goal is based on a reasoned expectation, any difference can, at the very least, be explained. The trust that results by treating the sales team with integrity will build a sense of loyalty and partnership that ultimately translate into a benefit to those who matter most—customers and clients. If the right person for the job has been identified and if leaders are communicating well (a topic to be addressed in the next chapter), the benefits of inclusiveness far outweigh the risk.

* * *

Understanding this is of critical importance to all the principles that follow, so permit me to reiterate the concept. The key issue is *how* to successfully establish realistic expectations in the corporate endeavor of attaining the business's objective (its reason for being). This very process, the *way* in which "realistic expectations" are determined, has been a great frustration for many of the sales people I have trained over the years. Good sales people believe that goals are *not* a necessary evil in business; they are a necessary good. The only issue that might arise revolves around the means used to arrive at the goals, not the need for them. When leaders choose to include those who are in the field in their intelligence gathering, even if there is a differing of opinions about how "realistic" is defined, the respect shown builds trust, especially when the right persons are in the job. The improved sense of partnership created within the sales force translates very positively to the consumer, resulting in further opportunities for success. (By the way, customers and clients can tell quite easily when the sales force is satisfied; they view it positively, interpreting this satisfaction as evidence that the company is willing to attract and retain expertise—the very thing they as consumers want.)

* * *

The specific goals that you (or those in leadership over you) set for your particular business and industry are circumstantial. They are based on the unique aspects of your chosen markets, your specific products and services, and the competence and expertise of your sales team. The process used to establish these goals, however, should be principle-based and therefore unchanging.

Once the goals have been set, you as a leader must clearly communicate those goals and the reasons behind their establishment. For your team, these clearly communicated goals provide direction and confidence in the vision with which you are endowed. They also give your sales persons a sense of security that they are not wasting their time and energy by doing what they only "think" they have been hired to do, freeing them to give their best efforts.

The Tantrum Approach

I suggested at the outset of the chapter that not all goals are established on realistic or reasoned expectations, that some goals are established irrationally. It is apparent that the unreasoned approach, when it is used, is not adopted because leaders lack appreciation for the benefits of clearly defined goals. It is rather the result of one or two misconceptions: either trying to build on an unattainable objective and/or the effect of a lack of proximity to the "field"— what is sometimes referred to as the "ivory tower" syndrome—in determining expectations.

Here is how the unreasoned approach to goal-setting is applied.

Someone in the corporate hierarchy determines that profitability is the objective and defines "realistic" solely on the basis of his or her desire that it be so, which leads to establishing his or her expectations; rationality is not his or her concern. He or she then decides that some arbitrary goal *must* be attained—arbitrary not because it fails to fit into their formula, but because there is no demonstrable reason to believe that it can be successfully achieved.

Let's say for example, that having been made responsible for setting goals and using nothing more concrete than "industry standards" or some other technical measurement and means, someone in management determines that this year's goal be a 15% increase over the greater of each territory's actual results or their last year's goal. Certainly this goal is mathematically sound and it can most definitely be inserted into a financial formula that would predict its bottom-line impact. As to feasibility…? Well, since management *wants* it, it must be feasible!

In an attempt to *appear* inclusive, even though the end product has already been calculated, input from the field is requested. If by chance the input were to suggest that more than the 15% increase would be possible, management would accept the greater increase in the goal. If, on the other hand, those in the field gave justifiable reasons to reduce the goal, they would be ignored and those suggesting such a possibility would be suspected in their ability to do their jobs (resulting in a self-propagating delusion regarding how to define "realistic"). After the "input" has been gathered, the predetermined goals are announced, sometimes under the cover of having been "jointly set," and everyone is encouraged to go "make the shareholders happy." In truth, no realistic feedback was sought, because no flexibility in the final goal existed, and those in the field know it.

A very interesting irony develops when this approach is used. Larger companies, those tracked by analysts, experience a greater negative impact on stock price when they miss an *unreasonable* target than if they meet a reasonable, though lower, target. So, in their attempt to please the stockholders, tantrum-style management has actually set itself and the stockholders up for almost certain disappointment.

Now, I absolutely believe that every business has the right to self-determination, to be run however its leaders deem best. My concern is not taking away their rights to do business any way they choose; my concern is helping sales managers be successful, and consumers, not shareholders, define success. (By the way, unhappy consumers will eventually lead to unhappy stockholders; happy consumers, in time, will always produce happy stockholders—the long-term key to a successful company is exceeding the expectation of the consumer!)

* * *

Let's take a look at the two significant weaknesses of this approach to goal-setting, the implications of those weaknesses, and then end with a reiteration of a consumer-driven approach to establishing expectations.

The first weakness is in attempting to build on an unattainable objective. Profitability is not a reasonable objective because it cannot be directly achieved. Profitability can only occur as the result or consequence of other actions—those actions should be the objective. No business exists for the shareholders, unless of course it is an investment company, better known as a mutual fund, in which case the consumers *are* the shareholders. Shareholders will be able, as business owners, to share in the rewards bestowed by consumers on those companies that exceed their expectations and create satisfaction. But the shareholder should never expect a company to make profitability its objective. History has proved that that approach does not work.

A critical implication of the profitability-first approach, in light of the topic at hand, is that when the objective is beyond the power of the team to achieve there is truly no reason to include them in any process of establishing goals. Management has no real motivation to be inclusive because nothing the team would have to say would matter, and again, the team knows it. Knowing that their input is not valued also drains the team of motivation, thereby making the attainment of the goals even less likely.

The second weakness: expectations are not established based on demonstrable reason—thus defying the very meaning of the word realistic. In this approach, expectations are more the result of desire—"I *want* profits"—than they are of reason. An expectation is defined as a confident belief; confidence must be rational if the expectation is to be realistic. The only rationale backing this type of sales goal is that the shareholders, or analysts, or some other "they" demand it, not a very substantial reason upon which to form a strategy.

The most important implication of this lack of reasoning is the assumption that today's efforts would somehow produce different results than they have every other time they were tried. This "insanity" results in a deep lack of confidence in management *and* a "do what you're told" mentality among the sales people. At the same time, management perceives the sales force as being an uncooperative, self-indulgent group of individuals. In a very short time, an adversarial relationship develops. Goals are imposed instead of agreed upon, turnover becomes commonplace, expertise is sacrificed, and the consumer's experience becomes dissatisfying.

Ultimately, all of this leads to frustration for management, underperformance by the sales team, and an unhealthy environment for consumers—no one wins. Having pursued profitability over consumer satisfaction, this approach to setting goals produces neither. What might have been achieved with the team engaged cooperatively will never be realized.

Bringing us right back to where we started: an approach toward goal-setting based in research, reason, and rationality, driven by the desire to satisfy the consumer. The changes that would be made to the unreasoned approach by implementing a consumer-based process would make a dramatic difference in the relationship between leaders and the sales team, as well as in the resulting sales performance.

By making the objective attainable and staying true to the leadership quality of direct involvement with those being led, management encourages a culture of mutual respect and cooperation and realizes the opportunity to excel. To do the first (establishing the objective) and stay true to the second (being an effective leader), leaders can and should ask these questions throughout the goal-setting process: "Do I trust the sales persons to do their jobs to the best of their abilities?" "Have I compared our goals to the company's objective to ensure that our efforts will be synergistic?" "Can I express my reasons for my expectations?" and "Are my expectations demonstrable?" The honest asking and answering of these questions will help you in your effort to be a true leader, building your company's good reputation and getting the most out of your team.

> As sales manager of Widget Enterprise, you have done research that suggests that your expert widget sales person, Ms. Smidget, should be able to sell an average of 83 widgets each month. In your inaugural sales meeting, you discuss Ms. Smidget's prior experience in the market as well as her learning curve regarding the specifics of your product and your emphasis on consumer satisfaction. Upon further analysis, the two of you agree that the annual goal of 1,000 widget sales is a realistic first-year expectation. To accommodate Ms. Smidget's needs, you will adjust the monthly goal to reflect a lower expectation early in the year and a higher expectation later in the year. Your decision to include her experience and to respect her need for time to build momentum makes Ms. Smidget feel even better about her decision to come to work for Widget Enterprise—which encourages her to let some of her friends in the widget business know what a great employer you are and committing to them to let them know when you are ready to add to your team!

From the perspective of fulfilled expectations and team building, the benefits of a consumer-driven approach to setting goals are remarkable. Knowing that the objective is within the power of the team to achieve makes it much easier and more natural for the goal-setting process to be inclusive and for expectations to be based in reason. Hope that the goal can be accomplished enables individuals to achieve what is otherwise considered beyond their reach. Believing that one's efforts will be appreciated and rewarded releases creativity and innovation: leading to the ultimate outcome—success!

When leaders view the sales team as a valuable resource, the conduit between the company's goods and services and the consuming public whose satisfied needs are the very reason the company exists, then goal-setting will be a healthy, inclusive exchange of vision and experience.

Effective communication is dependent on knowing and speaking to the perspective of each member of the team and in committing to attentively listening to what they say.

CHAPTER FIVE

Communication

When I consider the importance of communication, the lengths to which we, as a society, have gone in our attempts to facilitate it strike me. In the last twenty years alone, we have seen the means and sophistication of technology designed for communication skyrocket. From the integration of fax machines into daily business to the commonplace existence of cell phones for work and personal use to web-cams and email and blogs and "MySpace" and personal web pages: the list of ways to communicate with one another is mind-boggling. Whether it is text messaging on a cell phone or instant messaging on a computer, it seems we can't "talk" fast enough. But although we spend hundreds of dollars each month (to think we used to squawk about the old $25-a-month phone bill) on all of these avenues of communication, we are still faced with the age-old question: "did they understand what I just said?"

Though the devices and technologies have advanced, the process is as wrought with difficulty as ever. We use email, thinking that since it is in black-and-white there is less room for misunderstanding, and then create "emoticons" in an effort to add innuendo and feeling back into the conversation. We make simple assertions and then spend hours explaining what we *really* meant. We find ourselves misunderstood, misquoted, and misspoken and yet without any alternatives but to keep on trying to find a way to get our message across. When it comes to communication, the old adage "if at first you don't succeed, try, try again" rings true: when there is an idea that *must* be understood and a message that *must* be delivered, a means of communication *must* be found, no matter the challenges.

* * *

If it were simply a matter of desire and opportunity, communication would be a breeze, but it is far more complicated than that. Communication, like art, often becomes a matter of individual interpretation. Only unlike much of art, with communication there *is* a right answer, an intended message to be delivered. The challenge with communication begins with the fact that it is more than just an exchange of words. Communication is the effective conveyance of an idea that exists in one person's mind into the mind of another.

For the leader of a sales organization, the message is monumental—for within the ideas he or she must communicate reside the means of personal and corporate success. Sales managers must find an effective way to communicate. To do so they must approach successful communication as a skill and as a philosophy.

> After the first sales meeting with Ms. Smidget, you reflect on how it went; you are confident that you understood one another and that you left with fundamental agreement on the goal and the means to effectively achieve it, but arriving at that understanding was more challenging than you thought it would be. It so happens that the majority of her widget experience was gained in another part of the country and with a firm that not

only is not a part of your market but uses a completely different method for manufacturing widgets—not a bad method, just a different one. This difference in background and experience seems to have caused some confusion over what each of you meant when using industry-common phrases. For example, when you referred to the benefits of hydrothermalkinetitosis to the durability of widgets, she thought you were commenting on the cause of their resistance to fading when exposed to direct sunlight, not to their overall strength. And then there was her confusion over some of the colloquialisms that you weren't even aware you used, along with some questions you had about what exactly some of her phrases meant. These situations are resolvable and are by no means significant, but they start you thinking about other scenarios that might arise and reveal the challenges of communication. You want the communication between your sales team and you to be effective, not only now when the team is small but for as long as you are responsible for expressing vision and passion to them.

Communication Skills

What of communication as a skill? Are leaders familiar with or comfortable with the process and principles of communicating with the team well enough to make it happen? To this end (the improvement of communication between leaders and the team), there are several questions that need to be answered. Among them are: "What is communication?" "How is it accomplished?" "How can we be sure that we have been successful in our efforts to communicate?"

As stated above, communication is the transference of an idea or ideas from one person's mind to another's. Communication is more than just conversation: conversation happens whenever words are spoken between two or more people; communication happens when an idea is successfully transferred.

Communication is a complex process that consists of at least four distinct points where a breakdown is likely to occur. For an idea to have its genesis in one mind and its revelation in another, translation of the idea into words, tones, expressions, gestures, etc. (all of which elements I will refer to as "language") is required. The language is then expressed or "transmitted," received, and finally interpreted back into the form of an idea. Even in the most ideal set of circumstances, where both parties speak the same "language," there are enough possible distractions, interruptions, and misunderstandings for communication breakdowns to be an all-but-foregone conclusion. Worse yet, due to our various backgrounds and experiences, it is almost impossible for any two people to actually speak the same "language." Is it any wonder that effective communication is such a struggle, and skilled communicators are in such high demand?

As a leader, you face constant challenges in your attempts to communicate. But communicate you must. For you, the desire to communicate and the ability to do so effectively are vital to leading your team to their objective; therefore, every effort must be made.

> As you continue to implement your business plan and manage the day-to-day operations of Widget Enterprise, you are continually presented with evidence of the importance and difficulty of successful communication. It reminds you of having a sore toe: it seems like now that you are thinking about the possibility that communication might break down, you find yourself constantly "stubbing your toe" while trying to get your message across. Not only with Ms. Smidget, but with your production team, your vendors, your suppliers, your bank—virtually everyone with whom you interact.

You know that you want communication to go well, and you believe everyone else does too, so it is not an issue of motivation. One consistency does show itself: the more certain you are about your topic, the more often misunderstanding occurs. The times when you are discussing things that you know intuitively, with which you have significant experience, are the times when people seem more likely to get the wrong message. In mentally reviewing some recent conversations where the breakdown in communication immediately showed itself, you are able to confirm your suspicions. Your analysis reveals the following: There is a universe of knowledge specific to the widget world that has taken you decades to amass. This knowledge includes its own language, jargon, and lingo; when dealing with others associated with widgets, you tend to try to expedite communication by using these terms and phrases, believing of course that they will mean the same thing to others as they mean to you. Also, you are not in the habit of asking questions to make sure you are understood, and you do not typically verify compliance, trusting that others are conscientious enough to do their jobs well.

Communication failures are happening more often than you want. You are not sure how to resolve the problem, but you are sure that the network of mentors and peers with whom you consistently meet will have some ideas.

Principles of Communication

In light of the four points of probable breakdown, allow me to share what I have found to be four very helpful principles.

The first principle of successful communication: I must be thoughtful and purposed as I choose the "language" I use; I must make that choice with an understanding of the audience's frame of reference. In the initial step of communication (translating an idea in my mind into words, gestures, tones, etc. in order to express them to another), the ability for my audience to comprehend my meaning must always be my primary consideration.

The other day, my son and I were working on a project around the house. We were at a fairly critical juncture, holding a modestly heavy support piece that needed to be attached to a frame. I needed a little less slack on my end of the board to get a bolt to thread. I looked up at him and said, "I need it closer." He immediately and compliantly pulled the board toward himself. Fearing that I would lose my grip altogether, I quickly said, "No, closer!" Again, and with even greater force, he pulled the board toward himself. In desperation I yelled, "Closer! Closer to me!" The secret words "to me" made him understand what I wanted done. I gave him perspective; he suddenly *knew* what I was saying and pushed the board toward me. Now, the breakdown in communication was not because we don't both speak English nor was he incapable of doing what I needed him to do; the breakdown occurred because I had failed to consider his frame of reference. From where he stood, he *was* moving the board closer—closer to himself. As far as he knew, he understood me completely. Only by adjusting my words to account for his frame of reference did true understanding occur: the idea in my mind was transferred into his.

So it is with any audience. As the originator of the idea, I must consider the perspective of those to whom I am speaking, or face the probability of being misunderstood. Knowing the "language" of those with whom I am attempting to communicate is critical. And though this becomes exponentially more difficult as the size of the audience increases, I have no alternative—I must communicate if I hope to lead. So I must know my audience well enough to speak to their perspective. I must select the "language" that I have good reason to believe will enable them to understand what I have in mind.

In that same vein and describing the second principle I have learned, I must believe that the audience wants to receive and understand the idea I am trying to transfer. I must operate under the assumption that the team shares my desire for communication to take place. Not operating with this belief in mind propagates a very destructive attitude that can, and too often has, infiltrated a sales team: that leaders and sales persons are adversaries, not team members working to accomplish the same objective. If this attitude exists and is not corrected, no amount of communication skill will make a difference. If I begin an attempt at communication doubting the good intent of the listeners, an already difficult process becomes even more constrained.

To encourage communication with the team, I must approach them from the mindset that we are on the journey together, that success is our goal, and that the pursuit of the consumers' satisfaction defines our mission. Doing so is often the difference between failed and successful communication—it is like the difference between swinging through and bunting; I *may* not hit a home run when I swing through, but I *can* not if I don't.

Admittedly, a team member could be of the frame of mind that he or she does not want communication to be successful, but that will be the exception not the rule when the right persons are on the job, and a matter for individual coaching when it is the case.

The third principle of successful communication is feedback. I can only know that communication has occurred if I ask for and receive specific feedback, the most valuable of which is changed behavior. I must make obtaining feedback a priority both in regards to my message and to my methods—consistently requesting feedback and responding to what I receive. And I must verify understanding by observation.

After all is said and done and I have given my best effort to the process of communication, only by observing changed behavior can I be absolutely sure that my message was received and my idea transferred. Acknowledgement, assent, and agreement are excellent, but the only undeniable means of ensuring that communication has happened is observable change. In the illustration above with my son and me, his actions provided me clear feedback of when communication had or, for that matter, had not taken place.

Thus, I have learned to make it my practice to include some measurable form of action in response to any important message I deliver. For example, when, as a sales manager, I would ask my team to focus on professional expertise and development, I had to do more than just talk about it in generalities; I needed to give them specific courses, suggested timelines, and then meet with them to observe and discuss progress. Or, when someone on my team struggled with identifying client needs, it was never enough for me to talk about the importance of profiling and for them to commit to doing a better job. I also had to review their profiling forms and their profiling process—and that review had to cover enough cases to enable me to recognize changes to their methods in response to my coaching. Ultimately, it was only these observed actions that *proved* my message had been received.

The fourth principle of communication that has been of great assistance to me is one that has been used by the great communicators of every era. I must begin with a known reality to introduce a new concept, using the familiar to bridge the gap to the unknown or unfamiliar. For example, in working with a farmer with little investment experience, I could use the familiar benefits of crop rotation to explain the unfamiliar effects of economic cycles on investment performance, making it possible for me to transfer a new concept into his mind.

Another example might be describing to a sales person, whom I know to be a big baseball fan, the benefits even the best hitters get from having the mechanics of their swings watched by a coach. I could use this illustration to bring confidence to him or her in the benefits of having me watch him or her in action, assessing his or her skills, and reviewing the fundamentals of proper sales.

As these two examples suggest, for me to effectively apply this principle I must know my audience. And just as sales persons must profile their potential customers and clients in order to identify their needs, I must profile each member of my team to identify his or her frame of reference. With this knowledge, I can effectively introduce new concepts by bridging from what they know to what I want them to understand.

> After discussing your problem with one of the best communicators you know and attending a couple of workshops on communication, you are confident that you have identified what you need to do differently to improve communication with those with whom you work. As a start, you establish as a personal goal, profiling all twenty-three of your employees to become familiar with their frames of reference. You reason that even though you don't have direct contact with each of them, the process of learning their frames of reference will help you develop your communication skills and reinforce the importance of the process. You may know what their résumés tell you, but you now recognize that you need a three-dimensional perspective. Better understanding of the points-

of-view of those whom you have hired will enable you to adjust your language to facilitate communication.

You also are committed to improving the feedback process, especially when the understanding of what you have said will make a difference to your business's ability to succeed. This improvement will come in two distinct behaviors: you will make it a habit to ask good check questions after giving instructions or making recommendations, *and* you will include specific, measurable actions for your team members to take and confirm their understanding by measuring the task's completion.

These changes return immediate benefits. The occasions of misunderstanding, and the resulting frustration and ineffectiveness, are a fraction of what they were. You also notice an additional fringe benefit: what was already a good place in which to work has become even more energetic. The slight cloud of tension that seemed to overshadow meetings and even one-on-one coaching sessions has lifted and been replaced by a new confidence that stirs innovation among the entire team!

Communication as a Philosophy

The other key to successful communication is having a philosophy that recognizes its critical importance. By definition, a philosophy is a way of thinking, a collection of ideas, beliefs, and attitudes. At the root of the word itself is the idea of the pursuit of wisdom. With communication being the transference of an idea or concept, having as a philosophy the importance of communication suggests that every effort will be made to overcome any and all obstacles to the process of transferring ideas from one mind to another. For a sales manager this philosophy holds that it is necessary, in the pursuit of understanding, to continually express the objectives, strategies, and actions to which the team is committed... but it doesn't stop there.

By design, leaders have ultimate responsibility for the success of the team; therefore the onus for effective communication rests squarely on their shoulders. This means that it is not enough just to put value upon *saying* what needs to be said. Leaders must strive to transfer ideas as well, which requires that they also value and emphasize the process of verifying that the message was received. It is this second mindset toward communication that causes leaders the greatest challenges.

It is easy to believe that what I have to say is important and leave the results up to others. However, if I stress the importance of successful communication then I, as the speaker (the originator of the idea), must believe that the process of communication does not stop when the words are *spoken*, but when they are *understood*. The philosophy of the importance of effective communication espouses that I am responsible for my ideas being delivered in a way that enables them to be understood, and that I have to develop a mechanism that confirms understanding.

In formal settings, this mechanism might include exercises and role-plays that verify that the idea in my mind has been transferred to my audience. In a one-on-one coaching scenario I might observe behavior related to the message that I wanted to deliver as a means of confirmation. In an informal setting I would be more dependent on verbal feedback, with the hope that the concept had been successfully received prevailing, until such time as actions suggested otherwise. Under every circumstance, as the one who had the idea in the first place, it is up to me to find a way to determine that it has been successfully transferred.

By the way, this should never be taken to mean that understanding equates to compliance. There are certainly times when my audience will receive my message but not agree with my conclusions. For listeners to *knowingly not* take the actions I advocate still affirms the success of the attempt to communicate. The difficulty that accompanies this outcome is that the lack of compliance *might* also be the result of a breakdown in communication. Ultimately, the effectiveness of the means of feedback I have instituted will lead to my confidence in the effectiveness of my communications.

* * *

Though taking responsibility for understanding, not just speaking, is the central concept behind effective communication, enough speakers place the emphasis on what they have to say instead of on determining that understanding took place that we are all likely to have experienced ineffective communication. Whether in group-meetings or in one-on-one sessions, it is likely that we have all faced the frustration that comes from being talked to but not communicated with.

I, for one, have been part of numerous meetings, large and small, where the orator clearly thought that successful communication consisted solely of speaking. Whether the audience understood or not was not the speaker's "problem." As for taking responsibility to devise a means to measure understanding, well... that wasn't even in the speaker's universe!

I can almost excuse that behavior when it comes to communicating with a group; there are so many perspectives, so many "languages," so many challenges to successful communication. But if the message is important enough to take the time to say, then the message is important enough to take the time to make sure it was understood. An effective speaker will always include a method to ensure that the message was not only transmitted but also received. (Effective speaking should not be confused with entertainment; if the purpose is simply to entertain, there is no significant message being delivered, no behavioral change to influence and therefore no serious reason to obtain feedback.)

Along with the challenges of communicating in a group setting, I also have heard many stories from sales persons who, after a face-to-face meeting with their sales managers, have spent days, that turned into weeks and then into months, not exactly sure of what was expected of them. This confusion was not because management had not "told" them what to do, but because management didn't value or possibly understand the nature of successful communication well enough to verify that understanding had actually taken place. "Why didn't the sales person ask for clarification?" you may ask. Because either they thought they knew what had been said, it only becoming apparent later that they were mistaken, or they didn't want to appear "stupid" by asking questions.

Speaking of: I once heard a sales manager assert that there were no "stupid questions, only stupid mistakes," intending to give his sales team a sense of confidence in coming to him if anyone should have questions. He wanted open communication—and in his mind, this was an effective way to make that clear. Unfortunately, what resulted was an apprehension about taking action for fear that a "stupid mistake" might be made, leading to a serious lack of creativity and innovation. The idea in his mind was certainly not what ended up in theirs! Instead of his comment producing what he wanted, it did pretty much the opposite. But the real problem was in the fact that since there was no established method for feedback, it took some time before he was able to isolate the cause and correct the resulting downturn in effectiveness.

That story may seem unusual, but in my experience it really isn't. Many of the causes of the biggest misunderstandings between leaders and their sales teams are no more glaring than the communication breakdown described here. There was a desire to communicate a message and the means for doing so, but there was a breakdown—something slipped in the process of transference. And since no means existed to verify understanding, the problem persisted and compounded.

* * *

Leaders are responsible for expressing themselves in a way that is understood by those to whom the leaders are speaking. Leaders need to communicate, not just converse . . . leaders need to lead. Talented sales people want to know what is on their sales managers' minds, and they get frustrated when they have to guess what it might be, when it isn't articulated clearly. Even when both parties want communication to succeed it takes purposed steps for that to happen; it is the leader's role to take those steps.

I mentioned this earlier: leaders must look at communication like nourishment; no matter how well the table may have been set yesterday, the team will need to be fed again today. No matter how clearly priorities are stated today, enough interference, distractions, and contradictions will happen over the course of the next week (if not day) to necessitate a refresher. To not do so risks a failure in communication and the resulting frustrations, disorganization, and ineffectiveness. On the other hand, I have yet to hear a single complaint of a sales manager who communicated *too* well!

As a leader, you must be convinced that clear communication of the principles of effective sales will lead your team to success. The worst thing that can happen if this communication is neglected is failure. The worst thing that can happen if this communication occurs is confirmation of the means of success and heightened confidence among the sales persons that their efforts are valid.

On the Receiving End

Before I leave the topic of communication, a look at the leader's responsibility to *hear* what his or her team member is saying and to receive what is being communicated is warranted.

The focus of this chapter has been on the responsibility you as a leader have to place value on the importance of communication, to know your audience, to choose a "language" that you have reason to believe will be understood, to obtain feedback throughout the communication process, and to include the expectation of specific behavior as a part of the message in order to verify understanding. But what about when you are on the receiving end of the conversation? What can you do to facilitate communication when the idea begins in the mind of one of your team?

While it is true that the person who begins with the idea or concept must take responsibility for the success of the communication process, one of the overriding principles of leadership requires that you provide a good example of the skills your team must master in order to succeed. One such skill is good listening. Sales people, in their endeavor to identify consumers' needs, must have the ability to *receive* communication from their clients and prospects. Sales people must be good listeners; they should be able to see the skills necessary to be a good listener demonstrated by their managers.

Previously I encouraged you to believe that those to whom you are speaking want to hear what you have to say—that to believe otherwise becomes a hindrance to building your team. In reality, however, it is likely you have been involved in conversations where the hearer wasn't interested in listening or receiving. As frustrating as that can be for you as a leader, it is even more devastating to experience it *from* a leader. For the speaker to be in a position where he or she is reliant on someone else and then to have that person fail to show a desire to hear what he or she had to say is very demoralizing. My guess is that you know first-hand that this is true; that you too have had someone you looked up to or to whom you reported fail to hear you when you really needed to be heard—use that experience to help motivate you to be the kind of listener your team needs you to be.

As leaders it is vital to demonstrate, by the consistency between words and actions, interest in those things that matter to the team and to each of its members. It is this integrity that acts as the foundation of good listening: if the words say that we care, then the rest of the "language" (facial expressions, tones, posture, etc.) needs to as well. Under normal circumstances this may not be a challenge. When we have allowed ourselves the opportunity to prepare for a meeting, we can usually demonstrate the kind of consistency between our words and actions that is needed. For most of us however, it becomes more difficult when someone "springs" a problem on us, catching us off guard in the busy-ness of the day. I can't imagine that anyone who has been in a sales manager role for any length of time has not had the following scenario occur at least once.

There is a knock on your door. Even though you are right in the middle of a very important report, memo, email, etc., you invite the person in. They ask if you have a moment and you reflexively say "sure." Before you know it you are hearing a very detailed description of what is obviously an important crisis—at least to them. As you attempt to pay attention you find that you are still thinking about what you had been doing, struggling to not occasionally glance at your computer screen to review your work, even as the story your employee is telling you unfolds. You try to listen and you try to show that you are listening by an occasional nod of the head or an "encouraging" uh-huh, but the truth is you would rather not be having this conversation right now. You believe it is important to be accessible to your team but your sincere desire to be available, instead of being a positive, ends up as just the opposite.

In these situations nothing good can come. The team member knows that you are not really listening, you know that you are not really listening, the likelihood is that there is a bit of resentment building in you both, and under these circumstances there is certainly not going to be a reasonable resolution to the problem at hand! The importance of truly listening should not be overlooked; the focus of attention that good listening requires provides proof that leaders must strategically apply themselves to it.

There are several insights into what is needed to listen effectively that can be drawn from this simple illustration.

Attitude

The first is the significance of attitude. You must have an attitude that recognizes the value and importance of the speaker if you hope to listen well. While attitude can't directly be measured, it certainly can be displayed, and those displays are notable and measurable. (I suppose there are people who can do a good job of hiding how they really feel about something or someone, but they are not the type of people who should be in a place of leadership.) Leaders must understand that their attitude toward the person with whom they are communicating shows, and therefore they must make sure it is right *before* they start. Having the right attitude goes back to the idea of caring and caring is not something that can be trained; caring is a choice that leaders make.

Though making yourself available at all times may seem like a good way to demonstrate a caring attitude, in reality the complexity and demands of your job will probably require you to build-in some limitations. If your work-load is as hectic as most sales managers, you are more likely to display a caring attitude to your team by setting individual appointments or blocking out specific times to meet with them. In fact, having a structure to your day may be one of the best ways to demonstrate how valuable you believe your team to be—to carve out time where nothing else can interrupt evidences their importance.

Dedication

Which leads us to the second aspect of listening this illustration shows: to listen requires undivided attention and therefore dedication. I am not saying that you shouldn't be accessible, it's just that if you have an "open door" policy, you need to be sure to let your team know that there will be occasions when the only way you can give them your full attention is if you schedule the time.

Whether spontaneous or scheduled, you must give 100% of your focus if you are going to be able to listen. Doing things as simple as forwarding your calls, turning off your cell phone's ringer, moving to a round table without a computer or other possible distractions on it, and any other act that shows your commitment to listening will go a long ways toward facilitating communication. Those kinds of actions not only *suggest* to the sales person that they have your undivided attention, they make it much more likely that they *will*.

Sincere feedback

The last aspect of listening well is sincere feedback. This feedback will range from eye contact and body language to verbal expressions of interest and specific questions intended to clarify or confirm what was heard, leading to identifying and recommending indicated behavioral changes. The sincerity aspect is an outworking of the attitude mentioned above, to be sure, but it also reflects a cognitive rejection of what I call the "professional listener" mode.

If you have been in the sales arena for long, then you have likely been exposed to a number of courses, books, and seminars that have provided you with a list of "good" feedback questions to ask. And though I don't doubt the appropriateness or effectiveness of those questions, I do know that if they are used reflexively or repetitively they will *seem* insincere. For example, it was quite popular a little while back to use the phrase "what I heard you say was…?" in an effort to clarify a point in a conversation. Clarifying is a good thing and there is nothing wrong with that question, in and of itself. The problem comes when the same question is used repeatedly or in such a way as to suggest that it is a "technique" that is being applied. That kind of rote utilization of even the best clarifying question will impact the person being asked in much the same way that "have a nice day" does: they know that it meant something at sometime, but now it's just a cliché.

Sincere feedback has to generate from an attitude of caring and a desire to better understand what was said. There are any numbers of questions that can be asked to better clarify your understanding or even to confirm that what you thought was being said was in fact what was meant. Using a variety of questions will help to avoid the appearance of insincerity, but the best way to *not* appear insincere is to approach each point of feedback thoughtfully. Take the time to form the question or comment in the context of the topic at hand. Remember that communication is more art than science, what works one time may not work the next. Keep your goal in mind—understanding—and draw from your own experiences, and you can be confident that the feedback you give will encourage the process of effective communication.

———◦◦———

Communication is more art than science. The language that works one time or with one person will not necessarily work with the next. That challenge however, does not in any way release leaders from their responsibility to communicate.

Imparting vision, direction, and perspective is essential to accomplishing any worthwhile objective, and communication is the sole means. Leaders must believe in the importance of communication and be willing to apply themselves to the development of the skills necessary to communicate effectively. By knowing the team, thinking of their perspective when choosing the "language" used, believing in their desire to receive the message being transmitted, and using concepts that they are already comfortable and familiar with as the bridge to new ideas, leaders are given their best opportunity to experience successful communication. By building measurable responses to the communication process, they can verify that communication truly has occurred.

In facilitating the team's success, a Sales Manager must believe in the team's value, assist them in overcoming the obstacles and challenges that arise during the sales process, and provide them with an environment that encourages innovation.

CHAPTER SIX

Give Them What They Want

So far, we have examined the first five leadership principles of sales management: from understanding the primary objective of the business in general and sales management in particular to identifying real market opportunity; from setting and communicating good goals founded on realistic expectations to knowing and acquiring the right person for the job. We know what needs to be done, generally and specifically. We have the right team in place to effectively satisfy consumers, matching the business's solutions to the consumers' needs. And we understand how important it is to communicate with the team successfully.

The remaining aspects of the sales management model are: keeping the team you worked so hard to build intact, developing their level of expertise until they are the best they can be, and, when necessary, letting go of those team members who, despite your best efforts, prove not to be the right persons for the job.

Keeping the team intact is the focus of these next two chapters. This chapter covers identifying and satisfying the needs of your team, enabling you to get the most from this valuable resource. Chapter Seven provides a thorough examination of the principles behind designing an effective compensation package, including sales contests and campaigns—what I call "creating a path of least resistance."

* * *

To create a work environment that facilitates keeping the team together, thus developing and retaining expertise (remembering that consumers desire expertise in their buying experience), the starting point for sales managers is the belief that sales people are a company's most valuable resource. Because consumers have the final say on any and all business transactions, putting them in the driver's seat, the employees who are responsible for satisfying the consumers' needs must be viewed as crucial to the company's success. That foundational concept is laid out in its entirety in my previous book, *Driven*, but in so much as it provides the backdrop for employee retention, the consumer-driven sales model (CDSM) will be sufficiently defined and described below (a summary of the CDSM can also be found on page 31).

Let me begin by reiterating my working definition of a free-market economy: "an economic system that relies on innovation as businesses compete for the patronage of the consuming public." It is the fact that consumers have preferences and the freedom to pursue those preferences that requires businesses to find new, more effective ways to identify and satisfy those preferences, giving the business its means for success. In a free-market economy, consumers determine which businesses win or lose based on how well the consumers' needs have been fulfilled. Through their purchasing power, consumers, in essence, vote in favor of a business. Each sale is a vote of confidence in the business as well as the basis for an ongoing business relationship. In this economic system, success is achieved by having the necessary skills and aptitudes to identify consumer needs and to satisfy those needs, with appropriate goods and services, more effectively than other businesses in the chosen market. It is by no means a perfect system, but if the goal is to encourage creativity and innovation in the pursuit of solutions to the material needs of a society, no more beneficial system has been found.

Our free-market economy benefits the consumer by forcing businesses to continually improve their products and processes in their ongoing efforts to earn trust and patronage. It benefits business by providing a clear path for success, thus freeing them to devote their resources to those activities that produce it. Because consumers want to be in a place where the satisfaction they experienced can be *repeated* the next time they have a need and can be *shared* with others, sales persons and the companies for which they work are rewarded with loyalty and personal referrals as they create consumer satisfaction. Seen from the other side, if a company (or any of its sales persons) decides that consumer satisfaction is not important to the company's long-term success, that company will experience the power of the free market—it will have fewer and fewer consumers to dissatisfy.

The CDSM recognizes that businesses exist solely to satisfy the legitimate needs of consumers; the delivery of that satisfaction—in the form of products and services—is the responsibility of the sales team. It also acknowledges that sales people, as the conduit between the company's solutions and the consumer's needs, are a business's most valuable resource. Consumers want, even demand expertise in the sales process—especially if they are spending significant resources on the purchase; the CDSM holds that having and keeping expert sales people is a sure means of success because it ensures true sales: recognizing what consumers want and giving it to them. Lastly, the CDSM recognizes that consumers are generally pro-business; as long as businesses are focused on meeting and exceeding consumers' expectations, consumers are willing to return loyalty and referrals as their reward.

In this philosophy of selling, true sales is made up of the following four phases and the required skills to effectively complete them. (For now, I will only identify these phases. I will address their specific challenges and how you as a leader can assist your team in developing the skills needed to effectively execute these phases later in the chapter.)

First is *prospecting*, which, in the CDSM, is more about building a good reputation than it is about "smiling and dialing"—though phone skills are definitely important. Second, *profiling* or identifying needs, which draws from the ability to understand and empathize with consumers. Profiling also requires the expertise to "ask the right questions" and the commitment to truly listen to the consumer's answers. Next, *presenting solutions* or satisfying the needs identified, which requires exceptional communication skills as well as an ongoing knowledge of available solutions. Finally, *promise-delivery*, which is sometimes referred to as the service after the sale and is defined by the qualities of expertise, professionalism, integrity, trustworthiness, the belief that what they (the sales persons) do matters, and putting the needs of the consumer first.

Believing in and exemplifying the CDSM sets the pace for excellence; the CDSM is an approach to selling that engenders repeat and expanded sales opportunities. By encouraging the team to become experts at identifying and satisfying consumers' needs from a motivation that centers on the consumer as being the sales team's real "employer," they are provided with the very best opportunity to build lasting, successful careers.

> Widget Enterprise has grown beyond your most optimistic forecasts, requiring you to expand not only your production

capacity to keep up with rising demand but also your sales team. This rapid growth has stretched you in many ways, and though you are not complaining, you are definitely aware of your need to bring Ms. Smidget "up to speed" on the responsibilities of sales management so that you can focus your attention elsewhere. Along with the excitement of success comes another surprising event: your middle child, who recently graduated from college with a business degree, has developed a sudden interest in being a part of your business. Your philosophy dictates that he learn the ropes first-hand rather than ride your shirttails so you give him the choice of focusing on the manufacturing, the business accounting and finance, or the sales departments of Widget Enterprise. Because of his naturally outgoing personality, you are not surprised when he chooses sales.

This creates the perfect opportunity for Ms. Smidget to develop and hone her leadership skills while at the same time relieving her of the developing backlog of prospects. In fact, things are going well enough that you suggest to Ms. Smidget that she let her industry contacts know that you will be recruiting and hiring another sales rep (in addition to bringing your son onboard)—informing her at the same time that you would like to begin transitioning her into the sales manager's role.

Leaders must chart the course; prepare and equip the team to navigate the course; exemplify the right way to run the course; and enable them to finish the course successfully. The consumer-driven sales model is the compass that keeps the team on course. The goal of any sales team is satisfied consumers—not sales, as some might suggest. Sales are a consequence, not a goal. The more satisfied the consumer, the more loyalty he or she will have for the business and the team. This loyalty is shown in continued patronage and recommendations to friends and family members who express similar needs.

By serving the needs of the consumer, the team will have the opportunity to be rewarded; by knowing what the consumer needs and by giving it to him or her, the sales person is positioned to have his or her own career needs met. The reward of a job well done is the opportunity to have another job to do. This philosophy recognizes that the consumer is first and foremost. Because of the consumer's priority, sales people—those whose responsibility it is to act as the intermediary between the consumer and the business—are regarded as the company's chief resource. This corporate mindset results in an environment of security and contentment among the employees, leading to the ongoing development of expertise, which produces more and more consumer satisfaction in an ever-widening spiral of success.

Clearing Obstacles

With the right environment, the opportunity for building and keeping a successful sales team exists. Experiencing that opportunity requires significant effort on the part of leaders. In my years in sales and sales management, the unanimous number one request from my team members can be summed up in the following statement: "clear the way so I can succeed." They didn't want me doing their jobs for them, they just wanted to be sure that any of the hindrances to success that could be removed, were. The importance of my ability as a leader in fulfilling that request can be illustrated with an example from football.

Personally, I was not particularly athletic growing up, and though I enjoyed sports, I was more inclined to academics and the arts. My sons are a different story. Those old enough to express an interest in a sport or two (or three) have all, eventually, settled on football. At last count, I had one son playing college football, a high school graduate who played three years of prep football, two playing at the high school level, and a pre-teen playing in an organized, full-contact fall league—an accumulation of twenty-four seasons of experience as a football father. Thus, I have become much more attentive not only to the overall objective of the game but to the tactics applied to achieve it, and even the impact of the individual player roles and assignments on the likelihood of victory. With the exception of my third oldest son, a senior in high school, my boys have focused on playing only defense: David, however, also plays quarterback. He is a good-sized, muscular young man at six-foot two-inches and 235 pounds with a good throwing arm, which means he is a threat to run as well as pass.

There are occasions when the offensive coordinator decides to call David's number for a running play or, for that matter, times when the defense forces a change of plans. The success of those plays depends not only on my son's ability to run but also on other players' abilities to block and clear "obstacles." If he gains significant yardage or, better yet, scores a touchdown, the cheers and recognition focus on him, but he would seldom, if ever, make it happen on his own. Yes, he must put out extreme effort, but without his blockers, he is vulnerable and exposed. If, during a game, they fail to do their jobs effectively often enough, he will begin to lose confidence in his ability to execute a successful play. Football (like sales) is a team effort; everyone's role is vitally important to the success of the entire team. Though what are known as the "skill" positions may get more of the attention, in reality they all must do their jobs better than the other team does theirs if they are going to win. Without the offensive line performing their tasks well, not only does the quarterback become ineffective, but also the hope of winning dims drastically.

As I see it, sales managers act in much the same capacity as the offensive line. If I, as a sales manager, fail to remove obstacles to my sales team's success, we have little hope of succeeding. There is no question that the "skill" players (my sales team) must put forth great effort and demonstrate high levels of professionalism and expertise if we are going to beat the competition. That said, I can make their jobs easier by doing mine well. If I take the time and put forth the effort to know what stands in their way, if I understand the typical hindrances that trip them up in the sales process and then find ways to eliminate those things, or at least minimize their impact, I am providing for not only their success but my own as well.

In my experience, there are obstacles particular to each of the four phases identified above. I will examine the most common hindrances associated with each phase and suggest those practical solutions that have proved helpful in my and others' careers.

> As a result of hiring your son and Ms. Gidgit (a previous associate of Ms. Smidget's in the widget sales business) you must provide training that covers the technical aspects of Widget Enterprise widgets as well as the skills needed to effectively sell them to the consumers in your market. You know that you and Ms. Smidget are excellent sales people, that you have the best interest of your clients and prospects in mind, and that you understand that the ongoing success of Widget Enterprise is based on the repeat business and personal referrals of your loyal customers. Much of what you do well while identifying and satisfying your clients' needs, you do intuitively. When you and Ms. Smidget discuss the need for training, she realizes that the same is true for her. You both know how to sell the right way and can certainly recognize it when you see it in others,

but neither of you is comfortable with breaking it down into the processes and steps necessary to equip someone else.

This realization sets you on the path toward identifying someone with whom you can work who has a philosophy and attitude that mirrors your own and the skills to develop, design, and deliver training that will help enable your new sales team to succeed. Your continuingly busy workload motivates you to assign the task of finding such a partner to Ms. Smidget. Your only involvement will be to sit in on the interviews with the top candidates.

After significant research by Ms. Smidget, she is able to narrow the choices down to two firms. Together, you two interview them and finally decide on a company whose motivation and approach fit your model and whose training modules can be customized to include the technical training along with integrated sales training you need. The one thing that tilted the scale in their favor was their insistence that they be allowed to provide a review of the skills needed for effective sales management first and that you and Ms. Smidget should participate. Though this puts a strain on your schedule, it relieves you of the responsibility of having to not only try to train your new sales team members but your new sales manager as well.

Prospecting

Prospecting is the term I use to describe those activities intended to acquire potential customers and clients. Prospecting includes all efforts to locate possible consumers of the business's goods or services. As such, it is the starting point of sales and the launching pad for success. Though the specifics of any team member's challenges and the corresponding solutions will vary greatly, here are a couple of examples of the most common prospecting obstacles—obstacles that your sales team is likely to need your help in removing or overcoming.

Common sense

The most difficult, and by far most common, challenge to prospecting is the initial marketing call.

In my experience, it doesn't really matter whether they are "cold," "warm," or "hot" leads; call reluctance is nearly universal. The reason behind this reluctance is not only quite simple, it is quite understandable: sales people think, "Since I don't like getting marketing calls, why would the people I am supposed to call like them?"

What your sales team is doing, often without even being aware of it, is applying one of the most effective keys to successful selling—they are using the principle of commonality. Commonality is the idea that we are more alike one another than we are dramatically different. The recognition and use of commonality is a very effective way to improve all aspects of the sales process—but it can also point out conflicts, requiring sales managers to be creative and innovative in their leadership.

It was while analyzing the marketing call—for which I was regularly asked to provide training—that my eyes were opened to the effectiveness and benefits of the principle of commonality. When utilized appropriately, commonality lends success to any marketing campaign and enables any sales model to produce reliable results. But it is indeed a two-edged sword. In regards to telemarketing, commonality suggests that if *I* don't like the intrusion of a "sales" call, chances are *no one* else likes it either—my experience on both sides of the phone confirms the validity of this suggestion. Consumers and sales people are not that different from one another—in fact, all sales people are consumers first (which in actuality gives sales people a huge advantage, if they will take the time to understand it). So what is the sales person to do?

As I began to grasp the implications of commonality I found myself faced with the sales person's dilemma: "if, during the course of my business, marketing calls are a necessary part of prospecting, and if the concept of commonality tells me that people don't want to receive my call, then I as a sales person am being asked to do the 'insane.'" Recognizing this dilemma put me in pursuit of a solution: I was confident that a way could be found to make marketing calls in a manner that would be acceptable to the prospect.

And so I set out to find it. There *are* phone calls that people don't mind receiving, even ones they actually enjoy receiving. What if we could effectively prospect while making those kinds of calls?

Believing that I am more like the average consumer than different, I began my research by considering the phone calls I actually like to get. From that inspection I was able to frame the structure and identify the elements of a "good call." For instance, I enjoy hearing from people with whom I have a relationship; calls from people for whom I care, and who I believe care about me, are always welcome. So relationship and caring are clearly foundational aspects of a good call. That is not to say that even those kinds of calls don't meet with a certain amount of resistance on my part, for they do. Even the good calls are an interruption, but they are an interruption I am willing to accept, for which I am even glad, because of my relationship with the person on the other end of the call.

From there, I focused on the types of business calls I like, or at least don't mind receiving: calls in response to a request, or in follow-up to a service or product purchase—those with a specific purpose behind them, especially if that purpose is in response to something I want. There are times when I am doing business with a company that they let me know in advance that I will be receiving a follow-up call. They care about the experience I have had with them, they are interested in my satisfaction, and they know that sometimes the depth of my satisfaction will not be revealed until some time after the purchase. When that call comes, it is not only expected, it is welcome. In fact, there are businesses with which I have a relationship whose calls I anticipate and I would miss if they were not made.

Finally, I compared any similarities between good personal calls and welcome business calls to determine if the marketing calls that sales people need to make could be formatted to line up with the "good" calls and to avoid as many aspects of the "bad" calls as possible.

What has resulted, through the several training workshops where these steps have been applied, is an approach to calling that has proved successful with most all of the frontline and dedicated sales persons who have taken part. We have designed a call that is founded on providing value (for new prospects) or highlighting an already provided value (for existing clients), that draws on an existing direct or indirect relationship, and that begins with politely obtaining permission to take some of their time by promptly identifying either the value we want to provide and/or the relationship upon which we are building. The recipient is given every opportunity to know that we believe that his or her time is valuable and that our call is either in response to a previous commitment or to a request that was made.

Here is an example of the start of a call to a new prospect that resulted from a referral given by an existing client that follows this model:

"Good morning, is Mr. Smith available?"

"Just a moment…could I ask who is calling?"

"Absolutely! This is Joe Livesay with CDE." (Pause.)

"Bob Smith here."

"Good morning Mr. Smith. A mutual friend of ours, Ms. Jones told me that you would be expecting a call from me regarding your company's need for Sales Training. I had a few minutes this morning and wanted to make myself available. Is this a good time?"

"It certainly is. Thanks so much for calling. Ms. Jones had nothing but good to say…"

The key to the success of this type of marketing call is its basis in the principles of commonality; the call seeks to reflect how we all want to be treated when we receive a business call. Because of that design, it is no surprise that these calls have been much more successful than the "smile-and-dial" approach in which I was originally trained!

There is a reason that "do-not-call" lists have become institutionalized. As employees of sales organizations, we have a choice: we can ignore consumers' preferences and alienate ourselves from them, or we can recognize what they want and give it to them, laying the groundwork for deeper and broader business relationships.

Referrals
The second most common obstacle to prospecting, and the one that if remedied successfully will make the marketing call even more effective,

is the "referral." Before developing my current model, I had seen and trained just about every imaginable script and approach for obtaining referrals—some better than others, some outright offensive, none as effective as I had hoped. The consumer-driven sales model, however, is a natural fit for obtaining referrals. As you may remember, one of the fundamental principles of the CDSM is that consumers are generally pro-business. Consumers want those businesses that effectively meet their needs to succeed for it is the best way for a consumer to have confidence that good businesses will be around to satisfy any future needs that might develop. The CDSM also holds that the typical consumer knows that loyalty and personal referrals are the best way for them to provide opportunity for those good businesses to succeed.

In other words, the typical consumer is making referrals, only on their terms not ours. As proof I ask: Who has been in some public arena—an airport, restaurant, conference room, or doctor's office—and overheard a satisfied customer making a referral? Comments such as the following: 'I noticed your windshield was chipped, I had to replace mine a little while ago and I used a company that actually came to me! It took them about an hour and they really weren't anymore expensive...' or 'I heard you say something about needing some good running shoes; well, there is a store about a mile from here where they take the time to fit you with the shoe that will be best for you. They are very helpful, know their stuff, and are worth the little bit extra you might end up paying.' I could go on, but this is a reflection of a couple of the actual conversations I overheard in just the last week or two. People are making referrals!

But the good news doesn't stop there. The recipients of the referrals almost unanimously expressed their appreciation for the recommendation— they now have reason to believe that needs they have will be effectively satisfied. Not only was a referral made, it was accepted as well. It makes sense; consumers would rather give their hard-earned money to a business or sales person who has been recommended by someone they know and trust than to a name from the phonebook. By using a company that was referred to them they have greater hope of satisfaction.

And I am no different. Like those I have overheard, when I have had a legitimate need satisfied by a business, I am very likely to give a recommendation to someone else when his or her similar need becomes evident. I make referrals, I make them gladly, and I make them often—to those businesses that meet or exceed my expectations. Also, when I have a need and someone I know recommends a solution I am not only appreciative; I am very likely to take advantage of their recommendation.

This *is* my first-hand experience, and that of most of the people I have asked, so why do so few sales people obtain referrals from their satisfied customers and clients? If the scenario you just read is true, then why is it so hard to get referrals?

For two reasons: we ask for them prematurely, *before* we have earned the right, before satisfaction is realized. *Moreover,* we fail to ask for them once consumers are ready to give them to us, *after* they have realized satisfaction. If satisfaction is a point on a timeline, asking for referrals before that point and failing to ask for them after that point are equally ineffective strategies; yet both are very common to the typical approach.

Again, the vast majority of the referral scripts and training sessions with which I have been involved advocate the "vote early and often" method of asking for referrals. The most common approaches consisted of asking every prospect, customer, and client for referrals at the end of every presentation, no matter how it went. In fact, there was a time when as a manager I would put more value in the asking than in the getting. The primary problem with this approach was that it ignored the possibility that the effect of asking might actually be negative, that it might actually erode whatever trust had been built during the sales process. The second problem with asking after every presentation; when referrals were not given (and they seldom were) they were not sought later on in the relationship, when it was more likely that they would be given.

Like much in the way of marketing, consumers have three choices in terms of how they will respond to a request for a referral. And, in much of marketing, the third option is seldom recognized: consumers will either respond positively, neutrally, or **negatively** to being asked—the probability of this last option caused me to rethink my approach. If the worst that could happen was that the consumer would ignore my request, then it made sense for me to ask for referrals whenever possible. But if it is possible, even likely, based on my research, that consumers will react negatively to a request for a referral made in the wrong way or at the wrong time, then sales teams must contemplate a more strategic approach.

It's about time... and trust

We have all likely heard consumers giving referrals to those they know based on a recognized need and their own personal satisfaction. We have also likely witnessed the recipients of those referrals express their appreciation for the referrals. So why the difference between the ineffectiveness of the typical sales person's methods when seeking referrals and the effectiveness of the unsolicited approach that most of us have witnessed, and have likely participated in ourselves?

It begins with philosophy. Though I will address the obstacles that are found in the presentation process itself, there is an aspect of the presentation, more specifically as regards the sales person's mindset toward the outcome of the presentation, which dramatically affects the chances of being given referrals. For receiving referrals to be a natural by-product of the sales process—as it should be—the sales person must *believe* that the most important end result of the presentation is earning the consumer's trust not getting his or her money. Often, a consumer will "close the sale" financially and yet still withhold his or her confidence. In fact, the near universality of buyer's remorse is a clear demonstration of the separation of the two: people will give a business their money before they give it their trust—making trust the rarer and more valuable commodity.

Consumers are expressing trust when they make a referral, trust based on their personal experiences. When consumers experience, after the purchase, what they were promised throughout the sales process, consumers develop a trust in the sales person and the business. Then, and only then, are consumers ready to risk their *own* reputations on the business's performance; then and only then will they willingly refer. Therefore, sales persons should wait until *after* the clients have experienced satisfaction before asking them to make a recommendation to others. Sales persons must ensure that trust has been earned and given before trying to "spend" it.

Think of your own experience. Do you recommend your doctor, dentist, mechanic, or other service provider? If so, why: if not, why not? Fully grasping the implications of the answers to those last two questions will give you and your team the formula you have been seeking for obtaining referrals. By providing the kind of satisfaction that will make you a trusted business partner, you will become a receiver of referrals; it becomes merely a matter of making the opportunity to confirm consumer satisfaction and *then* asking for referrals.

The opportunity to confirm that satisfaction was delivered will usually come at the end of the first follow-up contact. That is, as long as there are no issues that need to be resolved. If there are issues that need to be resolved, take care of those first. (By the way, studies have proved that confidence in a business is actually enhanced when a problem is resolved. In other words, the "problem" is not a problem as long as it is resolved satisfactorily.) The goal is consumer satisfaction; the natural by-product of satisfaction is trust, which, when realized can lead to referrals.

When satisfaction is realized makes apparent the other mistake made in the timing of seeking referrals. Not only is it possible to ask too soon, but it is also possible to not ask when the time *is* right. Remember the timeline: once satisfaction is reached, to not ask for referrals becomes the greatest hindrance to further success. Your team should be consistently making follow-up calls, ensuring satisfaction, and giving opportunity for the pro-business aspect of a satisfied consumer to express itself. If your team calls a client thirty, sixty, or even ninety days after solutions to the consumer's needs have been provided and reinforces the consumer's satisfaction, your team members will have a strong platform for asking for and obtaining a personal recommendation.

It is a real shame for a sales person and the business he or she represents to do everything right in the eyes of the consumer, and yet to miss the opportunity to be rewarded simply because the sales person neglects to ask for referrals.

* * *

Again, these are but two of the obstacles I have experienced in the area of prospecting; you may have others that your team brings to you. As a part of your leadership role, they need you to remove these obstacles so they will have a better chance at succeeding.

Profiling

Next is profiling. Profiling is the most critical phase of the sale for it is here that the potential client's needs are identified. Since businesses exist solely to identify and satisfy consumers' needs, identifying those needs effectively is the primary responsibility of any sales person. Obstacles to effectively identifying those needs are typically based on one of two concepts.

The first concept is more or less a matter of respect: the question is, "whose perspective matters most?" The answer should be an enthusiastic "the consumer's!" Though this may sound obvious, the way in which many sales persons behave declares their belief that it is their own perspective that matters most. They demonstrate this attitude by making a recommendation before gathering all of the pertinent information, by leading with a product or service, and by using their natural attributes disproportionately. Having two ears and one mouth, they should be listening twice as much as they talk during this phase. Time for leading the discussion will come, but while the focus is on identifying the needs, the sales person must be an expert listener; one who not only hears, but also understands. Respecting the consumer's perspective helps a sales person to dedicate his or her efforts toward becoming that kind of listener (for more information on listening skills, please refer to Chapter Five).

The second concept associated with the obstacles to profiling is very practical: have a set method for acquiring the pertinent information needed to make a recommendation. It is far too typical, even when a format is mandated, for sales persons to sidestep or shortcut the process. This complacency is often excused by the suggestion that consumers don't like to answer personal questions. Although I have experienced this in my career, it has been an extremely rare occurrence. I can think of two instances in more than ten years of client interaction; in both cases, it was more a matter of me not being the person with whom they wanted to work rather than their not wanting to answer questions focused on identifying their needs.

To put it into context, foregoing a thorough profile would be like a doctor prescribing treatment without first conducting a thorough examination and complete discussion of symptoms. If I saw a physician who *did* do that, I can't imagine following his or her prescription, returning to the office, or recommending him or her to anyone else! And yet how many sales people try to circumvent the "needs identification" process and jump straight into suggesting a product? How many sales organizations are more concerned with moving the "product d' jour" than they are about providing appropriate solutions? Is it any wonder that the average consumer is skeptical and even cynical about the sales process (and that includes you and me when we are on the other side of the transaction)?

* * *

For "sales" to be a respected trade, sales people must treat consumers with respect. The most dynamic way in which we, as sales people and sales leaders, can demonstrate respect is to take the time and make the effort to attentively know the people we are trying to help, determine their wants and needs, and establish which of the many available solutions will best satisfy those wants and needs. Profiling does just that.

There certainly are several formats and means that can be used for profiling, but whichever one is chosen, profiling expertly must be the priority. Each industry, institution, and individual will have its own nuances and preferences for the process. The core issue is one of consistency and thoroughness, not of methodology. Leaders need to help each team member find a way that fits his or her own personality while satisfying whatever corporate standards that are required—and then manage them accordingly.

A need cannot be proactively satisfied until it is known; profiling is the sales person's means of knowing the need and should therefore be given the time and attention its importance justifies. Specific questions must be asked because the specific elements of the need must be identified. In fact, consumers rely on the expertise of sales persons to develop the right questions, questions that will help in this identification. If consumers knew all the right questions themselves, they would likely be competent enough to find the solutions on their own too.

This reality leads me to one other vital point: sales persons must not assume that they know the answers to even the most basic of profiling questions and thus not ask them. Stereotyping or categorizing prospects prior to thoroughly profiling them may be efficient, but it is most definitely not effective—and the tendency to do so only increases with experience, if it goes unchecked.

If the sales person is wrong in his or her assumption, he or she runs a very real risk of losing the consumer's confidence. If he or she is right in the assumption, he or she loses out on the benefits that come when the client verbalizes the answers out loud—the power of the verbal contract that is created and its positive impact on the upcoming sales presentation. Whether they are right or wrong, making assumptions and taking short cuts in the profiling process undermines the development of trust between sales persons and prospects.

Presenting

The next phase of the sales process is the actual presentation. When a sales person does an effective job identifying the need or needs, suggesting appropriate solutions becomes quite natural—but natural should not be equated with easy. Presenting the right solution or solutions to identified needs requires significant skill and insight. The sales person must be well-trained and well-prepared if he or she hopes to earn the consumer's trust, thereby making the sale. Having the right solution is not enough. Knowing that it is right and proving that it is right are two totally different things—and yet a good sales person must do both. It is in these two aspects—knowing and proving—that the majority of challenges or obstacles to presenting are found.

Perfection is not an option
Before I tackle those two obstacles directly, there is a point I need to make: there is no such thing as a perfect solution—there is only the "best" solution available. Even "best" is a subjective measurement based on all of the elements included in the consumer's search for a solution, which means what is best for me may not be best for you.

Just for the sake of argument, let's suppose that at a given point in time a perfect solution was created. The facts are: markets, people, needs, and economies are in a constant state of flux and competitive solutions are constantly being refined and upgraded in an attempt to respond to those changes. This means that today's perfect solution, if it ever did exist, would no longer be perfect tomorrow.

Since the "perfect" product or service is a myth, businesses are left with designing the "best possible" solution based on identified consumer preferences. However, the lack of perfection should not be taken as license to shoehorn a customer into a solution just for the sake of booking a sale. Every effort must be made to match the customer's needs and preferences with the solution that most effectively brings satisfaction. Confidence that a sales person's assigned market has adequate opportunity (see Chapter Two) and that the right person was hired (see Chapter Three) should encourage the sales person and the leader to approach sales in this way.

The pursuit of the best solution then is the result of a commitment to the corporate objective: identifying and satisfying consumer needs. The company exists (or at least should exist) because the founders believed they had discovered a more effective solution than those already in the marketplace. Your sales team is the conduit between the consumers' needs and the solutions your company has designed.

There is one more component to add to determining the best solution, and that is the fact that I *know* that *I* am dedicated to finding what is best for the potential client. Though I may hope my competitors are likeminded, I can't be absolutely certain; that uncertainty *does* contribute to the calculation of which solution will, over time, prove itself to be most advantageous. Consumers have made it clear that they want to do business with companies which put consumers' needs first—knowing with certainty that that is my and my company's philosophy becomes part of the overall formula for choosing which solution is best.

What you don't know can definitely hurt you
Presenting the best possible solution and justifying its selection requires that the sales person possess sufficient knowledge of all possible choices available to the consumer. Under this general category of product/solution knowledge are three specific fields in which the sales person might find obstacles: company-provided solutions, competitor-provided solutions, and alternative solutions.

Permit me to give an example: if I have been asked to help invest a client's money and they would like to have exposure to the real estate market, I will need to have knowledge of the value and benefits of buying land and property directly (which would technically be outside of my industry), of the various real estate investment trusts and partnerships that are available in the market but I have chosen *not* to offer (competitor solutions), and of those real-estate-based investments that I *have* chosen to make available to my clients.

The fact that there are solutions that I have chosen not to make available, even though I could, is more a reflection of my inability to achieve expertise in all of the possible choices that exist than of their relative inferiority. I offer my clients, as an offset to a narrowing of choices; my sincere commitment to do only what is in their best interest. I again remind us that no solution is perfect, so I do not risk eliminating that option by reducing the choices down to a level that allows me to develop the necessary expertise to confidently make a recommendation. It is a recommendation, after all, that my clients are seeking.

And this holds true for your sales team as well. Every industry will have similar comparisons. There will be your own solutions, those that can be obtained only at your competition, as well as solutions (such as ignoring the need altogether) that are completely outside of your industry but still represent an option your prospects may consider. Each sales person must take the time and effort to gain a minimum of competence in the fields of alternative and competitive solutions. This can be accomplished by having your sales people do research independently or by adding competitive product training to your sales training menu. It is also within the scope of your role as a leader to assign or at least to encourage the team to share the knowledge they gain with one another. Ultimately, the purpose of this knowledge is to equip your team with an understanding of and confidence in the solution they will recommend.

* * *

Again, *competence* is the minimum standard for solutions outside of the company, but you should require *expertise* of those solutions your company designs. Expertise is specialized knowledge gained by either direct or indirect experience. When the consumer is being asked to spend a significant amount of his or her resources on your solutions, expertise is expected.

Your sales team must *experience* the solutions your company provides. If your company manufactures a tangible product, the sales team should observe the manufacturing process. If your company provides intangible products or services, your team must understand the scope, scale and significance of each and every facet and characteristic of them. To facilitate this, whenever possible, have your team acquire the solution they offer others. This can't always be done, for obvious reasons, but when it can be, I highly recommend it. In any case, your sales people must take the time to develop expertise in the solutions they sell. Not doing so represents the greatest obstacle for most sales persons in the area of the sales presentation itself. Not *knowing* for certain why their solution is best makes it impossible to *prove*.

When sales people are *not* confident in their depth of product knowledge, they are more likely to try to dominate the presentation, attempting to make sure they are not asked questions that they are not prepared to answer. Consumers recognize when this is the case. Consumers want to be able to ask whatever questions come to mind and to believe that the answers they receive are true and complete. Consumers perceive when sales people do not know the answer or are less than 100% convinced of the reliability of the answer given. When the sales person lacks product knowledge, it is a clear sign to the prospect that, even if his or her needs are understood, the solution he or she is being offered may not end up bringing satisfaction.

No matter how good consumers may have felt about the sales process up until that point in time, the display of a lack of product expertise during the presentation will erode consumers' trust and will motivate them to consider looking elsewhere for their solution. Providing the means and the opportunity for your sales team to be and stay knowledgeable is one of the best ways for you to help them present solutions successfully.

It's not what you say, but why you say it
The other aspect of presenting the best solution, once it has been identified, is proving or communicating the reasons for the selection to the consumer. Since I have already addressed the general principles of communication including speaking with your audience in mind, taking responsibility for the success of the communication process, and verifying that success by observable feedback in Chapter Five, I will direct you back to that chapter for further study. However, in addition to the general guidelines discussed there, I need to point out two specific issues that can become obstacles in the sales person's attempt to prove that the solution being offered is the right one.

The first issue reflects a refinement of the sales adage that customers "buy the sizzle, not the steak." This adage encourages the sales person to point out the "benefits" of a product or service—those things that might make a customer or client feel good—rather than to overwhelm the consumer with too many technical details. I certainly agree that consumers don't need to be or want to be as knowledgeable of a product's every detail as they expect the sales person to be. If that were their goal they wouldn't be relying on you and your team. However, that does not mean that the aroma of a good steak will satisfy their appetite; your solution has to have substance as well as appeal.

Describing benefits—making a client "feel good"—about the product in the short-term should not result in them being disappointed over the long-term. In other words, true benefits are those that create satisfaction in the customer not only at the time of the sale, but three to five days—even three to five months—later. It is not enough to just talk-up a solution, even if it is the right one, because after the initial excitement wears off, consumers need to have an understanding of why their purchase was right. They need to know *why* their decision is one that they should feel good about, and even more to the point, one that they should tell others about! It is because consumers know and experience the reasons *why* that business earns the consumer's trust—and it is trust that leads to loyalty.

In the past, my sales training focused on the differences between *features* (the facts about a product) and *benefits* (what those features are intended to give the consumer). In recent years I have added a third aspect of a product/solution: *reasons*, which are an explanation of *why* the benefits are important from the consumer's perspective. The refinement then is this: "customers *buy* the steak, *love* the sizzle, but *need* the protein" —not flashy I know, but that is the point. Customers and clients need to be given an understanding of why *this* solution is in their best interest, not just talked into believing that it is. This is likely to make the presentation a little longer, but it produces lasting satisfaction—and that makes it worth the time.

* * *

The second issue of communication specific to the presentation ties back to something I mentioned earlier in regards to the profiling phase: allow the prospect or client to verbalize even the most basic information about themselves and their needs. This is important because, for reasons that can be easily understood, most consumers enter the sales process defensively, even cynically. The sales person, allowing the consumer to express aloud their priorities, needs, and preferences during the profiling phase, creates a kind of verbal contract; what the consumer says takes on a measure of tangibility. It is very likely that sometime during the presentation phase their natural defensiveness will kick in. By reiterating *their* own thoughts and reminding them of the reasons *they* gave for wanting what is being offered, your sales person is better able to help satisfy their needs.

Let's say, for example, that you are the sales manager for a high-end replacement window manufacturer. While one of your sales persons is profiling for a client's needs, the client mentions, among other things, how expensive it can be to heat their home in winter and to cool it in summer. When, during the presentation of the solution, the client expresses some concern about the cost of your windows, your sales person, remembering the client's need, can use the insulation factor of your windows as a possible offset for some of their cost. The fact that less heat will pass through the new windows can save energy costs; the savings in energy costs can offset part of the price of the windows. Asking good questions and allowing the prospects to answer them during the profiling phase sets the stage for overcoming a concern during the presentation phase. If your sales person assumed that every old window was not energy efficient and therefore did not ask questions that encouraged the prospect to mention it, he or she would not be in as strong of a position to overcome the price concern if or when it came up.

As with any aspect of communication, the reiteration of their stated needs is more art than science and therefore must be done carefully. If it becomes or even sounds cliché or canned it will cause more harm than good. But if your sales team is sincere in their desire to effectively satisfy the consumer's needs, that sincerity will come through, the client's own stated needs will be recognized, and the sale will close on the client's terms—as it should.

Promise-delivery

The final step of the sales process is promise-delivery, which consists of everything that follows the commitment to buy and ensures that the customer or client experiences satisfaction. Promises that must be delivered include paperwork processing, follow-up calls, service after the sale, and anything else that was either explicitly or implicitly promised in any aspect of the consumer's interaction with the business.

The most immediate obstacle to promise-delivery is the proper completion of whatever paperwork arises from the sale—whether it is simply signing a sales receipt or filing complex legal contracts. Often overlooked or excused away because "good sales people" are not organized enough to do the paperwork correctly, here is where many business *relationships* are won or lost. As tedious and "unnecessary" as training on this part of the process might seem, it must be considered vital if you desire your team to reap the rewards of developing relationships based on their trustworthiness.

If you are like me, you have experienced the frustration that comes when someone with whom you have done business fails to deliver what was bought. Even if it is something as small as not "holding" the pickles or the lettuce from your hamburger, it undermines your trust and lowers your expectations (seriously, when was the last time you pulled away from a fast food window without first fully examining your order?). How much greater are the implications for your sales team? Failing to finish strong is the greatest risk your team will face in this phase of the sales process. To not dot an "I" or cross a "T" may be the difference between just making a sale and building a business relationship with its incumbent loyalty and personal referrals.

* * *

An appreciation for the rewards that can be gained during this step will go a long way to help motivate most sales persons to follow-through with their sales. Trust is the most valuable reward that a consumer can give to any business. There are times when a business will get a customer's money and not be given, or earn for that matter, his or her trust. A client trusts a business because he or she experienced integrity, the consistency between what was said and what was done. In other words, commitments made were commitments kept. Every promise generated, directly or by implication, throughout the entire sales process must be fulfilled, or the company and the sales person fail to earn unconditional trust.

Follow-up calls provide a wonderful opportunity to determine if the company has succeeded in delivering on all of its promises. Integrity can be confirmed, or if it is in jeopardy, the situation can be corrected. The most common obstacle here is the sales person's fear that a service need *will* be identified and that either he or she will have to resolve it or (and sometimes this is an even more frightening possibility for the sales person) trust that someone else will. By the way, whether the sales person trusts the service department or not is founded on the *consistency* between what the service department promises and what they deliver— the principle of integrity is constant.

As a leader, you must do all that you can to verify that those responsible for service in your organization operate with integrity as well. If you do not directly supervise your company's service department, team up with their leader to make sure you are working together to deliver all of the promises that have been made to your customers and clients. Since the life of the "solution," be it product or service, is significantly longer than the typical sales process, service after the sale is by far a more vulnerable link in the chain of integrity—you should do all that you can to ensure it is not a weak link.

This may seem like a sizeable amount of work and effort to expend "after the fact" of the sale. You may even ask, "Why take the time to do all of that?" Because once trust is earned, repeat business and personal referrals are, too. Doing the job right gives your team a chance to do it again and again! There is no greater job security than satisfied customers and clients; finishing strong ensures that outcome.

* * *

Though I did not intend to hit every possible obstacle or scenario in any of the four phases, the ones I have addressed represent the most significant, those that are brought up by sales people about 80% of the time when they are asked about the challenges they face during the sale. Having or developing the means to help your team overcome these challenges will go a long ways toward enabling you to retain the talented sales people you have worked so hard to recruit and hire.

> After attending the sales manager training provided by the company that you and Ms. Smidget identified, you came up with some agreed-upon, measurable goals; goals that the consultant will help you implement with your sales team. The first, since prospecting was not a real concern, is to develop a profiling form for your sales people to use and to design a program of accountability to ensure that it is being used effectively. When you and Ms. Smidget were doing all of the selling, profiling happened as a result of your experience and knowledge—there didn't seem to be a need to create a form since profiling was already being done. But with new sales people being added, and with the shift in sales manager responsibilities to Ms. Smidget, it was agreed that the time was right to codify the process.

The second goal that they will help you accomplish is the development of detailed product training—for Widget Enterprise's widgets and for the widgets made by your competitors. You understand that your unique product is not right for everyone who needs a widget. You believe that it is better, in the long run, for your team to send those who don't need your solution in the right direction for the widget that would satisfy their needs—when they do need the solution you produce, they will be back! Experience with your solutions as well as knowledge of the industry in general will equip your sales people to provide your prospects and clients with the opportunity to have the best widget-buying experience possible, which is of course your business's objective.

The third goal is the design of a comprehensive sales training program that will include all of the technical and functional skills as well as the "softer," more intangible skills (such as listening, asking the right questions, demonstrating to the prospects and clients their importance to your business, etc.), needed to do the job right. Though you and Ms. Smidget are experts when it comes to widgets and especially Widget Enterprise widgets and you are both very capable of selling them to prospects, neither of you feels confident in your ability to convert that expertise into a step-by-step training program—and yet you believe that is what will be needed for your new sales people to be successful.

All in all, you are very comfortable with the progress you and your team have made: you have been able to begin the shift of responsibility for sales management to Ms. Smidget, provided her with detailed sales manager training (which certainly didn't hurt you to attend), grown the sales team 200%, and are in the process of adding excellent sales training to your already significant menu of reasons why Widget Enterprise is a great place to work! After only 18 months, you are ahead of the plan in sales and have therefore been able to expand ahead of schedule, too. The reception of your product and process by the market has been very good; in fact, your only real concern is keeping up with demand—the development of your sales team, and especially of Ms. Smidget, will free up your time and energy to focus on that side of the business. You were pretty sure of the importance of hiring the right person when you offered Ms. Smidget the job as your first sales person; the last year and a half has proved how important that hire really was.

Releasing Innovation

There is one final need that I often hear expressed: though not specific to the sales process, this request represents a real frustration for sales people—and especially for those who are considered top performers. Sales people would like the freedom to make a mistake *without* reprisal.

Sales people need their managers to provide an environment that recognizes the importance of the consumer and thereby the importance of the sales team, to remove as many sales-process obstacles as possible, and to take the risk of letting them innovate. In some ways, this last need is a reflection of a leader's attitude of confidence in the team and its members, as well as in himself or herself. When a leader is confident in his or her role, strengths, *and* limitations, and believes that his or her sales persons are right for the job, he or she can relax the reigns… or even share them.

Having and showing confidence in your team eliminates the need for you to micro-manage and releases them to embrace an ownership mentality.

This mentality leads to innovation, which is vital for a business to be able to satisfy the ever-evolving needs of its clients.

Innovation, like ownership, is risky, but with the risk comes the opportunity for a reward significant enough to encourage you to take it. Let your sales team explore new ways to accomplish success, give them opportunities to discuss innovative alternatives to your current solutions—it is possible that they might just come up with some. The rewards of innovation include creativity, relevance, energy, improved reputation, and exceptional levels of employee involvement. To experience these benefits, you must be willing to share "ownership," to allow your team to take the risks of being extraordinary. Will mistakes be made? Absolutely, but so will great strides toward success!

If the right person for the job believes that he or she will experience the rewards of his or her efforts (a short definition of ownership), that person is freed to put out as much effort as is needed to succeed—in a word: to innovate.

The opposite mentality, one of indebtedness, encourages just enough effort to "pay the bills." If your team's thinking is based on the idea that the boss is watching so they better be "busy," there will be no innovation, no creativity, no life. If the team believes that they will be "hammered" anytime they make a mistake, they will adopt the mindset of a debtor.

* * *

As a leader, I was always on the lookout for innovators. This is especially true in the hiring process; knowing that innovation is a trademark of the "right person" and that finding the right person for the job allows me to focus on my other responsibilities.

As a free-market proponent, I believe in the value of ownership, and promote this concept whenever possible.

As a consumer, I will never choose a business partner—in particular one involved in an important transaction—that is steeped in an attitude of debt. I want an innovator. Even if the wheel he or she brings me is the exact same shape as every other wheel developed throughout history, I want the one *owned* by the sales person.

I want *life*, not *fossils*! That is important to me as a leader, because it is important to consumers.

Of the many responsibilities that you as a leader carry out for your team, one of the most critical is to know what they need to succeed and to give it to them; doing so effectively helps you retain the team you have built. Your ability to help them to succeed begins with your belief in their importance; your understanding and acknowledgment of the part they play in your and your company's success. It also requires that you know each of your team members' strengths and weaknesses, challenges and opportunities so that you can help them to be their best and to overcome the obstacles to their success.

The areas in which your team is most likely to face obstacles are those associated with the sales process itself. Though it is possible that these obstacles could cover a wide range, there typically are common challenges that apply to the majority of sales persons. Knowing these common obstacles and the means to remove them provides a good foundation. From there it is crucial that you identify any specific concerns each team member faces and develop a plan that will enable them to overcome their concerns. Your sales team looks to you like a running back looks to a pulling guard: prepared, equipped, and trained to remove any and all obstacles standing between them and success.

Along with helping them to succeed by developing their skills and abilities, it is important that you encourage them to embrace an ownership mentality. This is accomplished by allowing them to take the risks of innovation. Displaying confidence in the expertise and professionalism of your sales team will be a catalyst for exceptional results.

A company's core values are clearly expressed through the path of least resistance created by the compensation packages, contests and sales campaigns it designs; how a company spends its resources is undeniable proof of its priorities.

CHAPTER SEVEN

Creating the Path of Least Resistance

Although it was more than thirty years ago, I still remember my basic electronics class from high school. Not in every detail of course, but well enough to do the typical home fix-it jobs when needed, even rewiring a bathroom in our first house. What I remember most from that class is more in line with the characteristics of electricity itself—in particular, the fact that it "flows" and that that flow can be steered by setting up "dams" or resistance. Electricity follows the path of least resistance; it runs along the path that requires the least amount of effort. This fact allows for efficient and effective use of electricity, whether at the intricate level of microprocessors or the vastness of hydroelectric plants.

In truth, I find that people tend to follow the path of least resistance as well—though it might be better recognized as the path of greatest benefit. Because of this tendency, designing a path that has greater rewards and/or fewer obstacles than the other paths that could be chosen can be an effective way to direct people.

In the realm of sales leadership, recognizing this characteristic in your team and thinking of it in regard to compensation is extremely helpful, especially in the area of acquiring and retaining expertise. If you want an employee to gain expertise by focusing on a particular activity, the best way for you to make that happen is to pay him or her for that activity, commensurately if not exclusively. For example, if the ability to effectively identify needs and solutions is centered on knowing how many roundtrip flights your clients take each year, then paying sales people based on how frequently and consistently they acquire that information would ensure that they focus on that behavior. Or, if the most critical factor of your company's success is based on the number of prospects seen in a week, then founding the sales person's compensation on appointments-held would be appropriate.

These examples are exaggerations of course; no sales person's job is so simple that it consists of just one activity, but the point remains that compensation can be structured in a way that rewards specific behavior. If, or as, the priorities shift, compensation can be modified to either emphasize the new and/or de-emphasize the old. In other words, I can create and modify a path of least resistance that, through rewards and benefits, encourages those activities most likely to produce a satisfying experience for consumers. (By the way, the fact that compensation plans for sales persons are changed almost on a whim is quite different from the type of modifications I am advocating here, but I'll get to that in a moment.)

An example of how changes in an industry can be reflected in a system of compensation might be seen in your local wireless phone store. The cell phone industry is a dynamic, consumer-based business. As the industry has evolved and the hardware has become more sophisticated, spending time at the point of sale explaining and demonstrating the many features with which each phone is equipped has become a more effective method for creating consumer satisfaction. A *proactive* demonstration not only reduces the amount of time spent with each customer but also increases satisfaction and the resulting loyalty. If I were the owner of a cell phone store, that knowledge would motivate me to provide an incentive for my sales persons each time they initiated a proactive hardware demonstration. The details of such a compensation model are beyond the boundaries of this example, but I trust the concept is clear.

Sales managers can take advantage of the fact that consumers have needs and preferences by designing a compensation package that influences their sales team to do those things that enable them to expertly identify preferences and effectively satisfy needs. In fact, let me take it another step further, every compensation package out there is already influencing behavior. The questions are: is it by design or by coincidence? And is it the behavior that produces the desired results?

* * *

The typical compensation plan is a clear and undeniable declaration of a company's values and objectives. The areas upon which a business spends its resources are an indication of the business's core beliefs, in essence, the heart of the company. If a company really believes that consumer satisfaction is its primary means for success, the company will spend its resources accomplishing that end by designing satisfying solutions for the consumers' needs and by providing expertise in delivering those solutions. Since expertise requires specialized knowledge, which by definition can be acquired only from first- or second-hand experience, there will be an acquisition cost commensurate to how difficult the desired expertise is to attain.

In the monumental book *Wealth of Nations*, Adam Smith recognizes that labor, like any other resource, is subject to the forces of supply and demand. The two major supply factors he describes are "danger or risk" and "expertise or skill." The more dangerous a job, the more it will cost an employer to get the job done. The same holds true for the level of skill needed—the greater the expertise required, the more expensive the cost of labor. These factors may be offset by "soft" demand when fewer employers are in the market for a particular type of worker, but relative to all available jobs, those requiring the employee to take greater risks or to possess greater skills and expertise will be more expensive to fill.

What does that mean to leaders? To the degree that you want and need expertise to deliver your business's consumer-driven solutions, you must have a compensation plan that attracts *and* retains those with that level of expertise. This need for expertise becomes the baseline from which a compensation package can be adjusted or modified to encourage particular activities in response to changing needs and market conditions. Leaders must keep in mind that, as is true elsewhere, so it is with the purchase of expertise: you always get what you pay for!

Change for a Reason

I want to loop back around to the statement I made earlier regarding the frequency with which compensation plans are changed, especially in the sales environment. In much of the sales industry, it is not only expected that the pay plan will change every year, but that the changes will have a negative effect (read: less money for the same or more effort) on the team *and* that no "field level" input will have been sought regarding the impact of the changes.

Let me first state that employees, like consumers, want good businesses to succeed—it is in employees' personal best interest that good businesses do so. Secondly, the right person for the job will not want to be unfairly compensated . . . either way. These two premises form the foundation for the rationale that should be used when a compensation package is formed *and* for any changes made to it.

When a change is made to a compensation plan that results in lower benefits being paid to the sales person who is being asked to continue providing the same effort and skill, the clear message is "you are not as valuable under this compensation package as you were under the last one." This again reflects a fundamental flaw in thinking. Each year a sales person, who is the right person for the job, gains *more* expertise, making him or her *more* valuable to consumers, not less. A company that understands the real value of expertise in providing consumers with the satisfaction they seek will demonstrate that conviction through the compensation plan, rewarding and retaining those who have developed expertise.

> You have always understood the value of labor: you have known since the outset of Widget Enterprise that you will get what you pay for in all of the resources your company needs—employees are no different. With Ms. Smidget, you were confident in her sales ability as well as in the abundance of opportunity. Because of your confidence in those two areas, you implemented a compensation plan that focused primarily on commissions. The changes that you are currently executing require that you take another look at your compensation model. The first item for review is Ms. Smidget's compensation. Obviously, her shift to management, even though she will retain some sales production opportunities, will require that her salary be restructured. Your desire to demonstrate her value on one side and her inexperience and the market forces on the other should give you a good set of boundaries from which to develop her entire compensation package.

The second item is a little more difficult, partly because you are adamant that your son is not given any favored treatment, and partly because of the changes in the dynamics of the opportunity. You know that there is plenty of market share still available; if there weren't, you would not have added both positions. But you also know that as you capture more of the total widget sales, the incremental increases will be harder to come by. You are dealing with one inexperienced and one moderately experienced sales person: creating a compensation plan that provides them each with sufficient income to allow them to develop, while also providing enough incentive to stretch their comfort zones, will take some time. They were hired under a ninety-day training salary with the understanding that their post-training compensation was still in the works—for Ms. Gidgit, her confidence in her friend and your reputation as a great employer made that an acceptable arrangement. For your son . . . well, the same could be said.

The Path of Greatest Benefit

Assuming that the business is willing to design a compensation program that rewards expertise, how is it done? How do sales managers participate in the process of creating or modifying a pay plan? For that matter, how can a sales leader know that he or she is rewarding the right skills and expertise?

Leaders, to help answer these questions, can tie many of the principles presented in previous chapters together. As I discussed in the chapter about recruiting, a sales manager must know the complexity of the skills that are needed to do the job, this knowledge will help determine the basis for compensation. By following the principles found in the chapter on identifying opportunity, a sales manager can be confident that the commission aspects of the compensation plan are designed correctly. As a leader applies the principles of effective goal-setting and reasoned expectations, he or she can have the assurance that the overall compensation package will encourage the activities that produce success.

This is not to say that designing an effective compensation package is easy. There are many factors to a compensation plan; analyzing how each element is affected by the others to produce the desired "path of least resistance" is itself an area of expertise that must be developed. Leaders can dynamically demonstrate the value they bring to their businesses precisely by how effectively they develop this expertise. By leaders recruiting the right person for the job, providing them with the circumstances needed to develop the expertise that leads to success, and compensating them in accordance with their expertise, they have created an environment that can exceed expectations through exceptional consumer satisfaction.

When a company values expertise, professionalism, communication skills, and the other core aptitudes and abilities found in successful sales persons, the company will find ways to measure those attributes and reward the team for demonstrating them. Believing that expertise is worth paying for will be accompanied by recognizing and rewarding expertise. For example, knowing that communication skills are important to the selection of the right person for the job would be the first step. Finding an effective means of measuring its use and application by anyone on the team would come next. Lastly, creating a compensation package that effectively rewards that behavior would naturally follow.

A compensation plan creates a path of least resistance, a path of greatest benefit. It demonstrates more clearly than any other corporate document the values and beliefs at the business's core. No matter what leaders say about their desire to satisfy the consumers' legitimate needs through the provision of effective solutions, the compensation plan is an undeniable, tangible declaration of what is truly believed.

Knowing which skills and the associated activities that best achieve the overriding objective is basic to creating a compensation plan that rewards them. Clearly measuring those skills and activities ensures that sales persons will be fairly and justly compensated. This will take time and effort not only when the team is first formed, but also at least annually to respond to changing markets as they affect consumers *and* as they affect the cost of acquiring expertise. Note that I am not advocating fewer compensation changes, just a different rationale from which to devise them.

Sales Contests

The other area of creating the path of greatest benefit that I want to address is contests. Along with the overall compensation plan, every sales organization about which I have any knowledge has adopted sales campaigns or contests as an ancillary means of inciting or at least directing behavior. Though I believe sales contests have their place and can be a very positive aspect of overall compensation for desired behavior, too often they are misused and ineffectually designed.

The elements of an effective sales contest include alignment with the primary objective; measurable, attainable goals; deciding to be inclusive by using a benchmark or exclusive by creating competition; and clarity in the mind of leaders about whether the contest is intended to reward existing behavior or provide an incentive significant enough to actually change behavior. A specified time frame and a reward commensurate to the desired actions are the two final components.

Let me give you a fairly detailed explanation of how I would apply these principles in designing a sales contest.

Activity based

First, any contest I design would have to be centered on an activity or activities that help achieve the primary objective of identifying and satisfying the needs of consumers.

One of the most commonly made mistakes regarding contests happens right here. Many sales organizations design contests based on results or effects instead of on measurable actions and behaviors. This is a mistake on two fronts. First, it reveals a faulty objective—sales—instead of a focus on the behaviors that result in client satisfaction. Second, it attempts to reward what cannot be controlled—meaning some sales persons doing all the right things are overlooked and others who accidentally stumble into a big sale (and we all know that that can happen) are rewarded. When that occurs, what is reinforced by the contest is exactly what you as a sales manager *do not want!* You want to take "chance" out of the formula and focus instead on being successful by directing your team to do the things that consumers want done, activities that can be relied upon to produce success. To get the most out of a contest then, it would need to be activity based, focused on a behavior or behaviors that produce consumer satisfaction.

Measurable and reasonable

Next, depending on the market for which I am designing the contest and the particular activity being emphasized, I would determine the specific goal that I want my team to attain. Since I must be able to accurately measure progress toward the goal, and it must be reasonably attainable, I would need to choose the goal carefully. It must be measurable because there is nothing that will be a bigger **disincentive** than for those participating in a contest to feel that they are being treated unfairly. If progress cannot, or is not, accurately measured, results are considered subjective, which translates to "unfair." The goal must be reasonably attainable because without hope of accomplishment people are not likely to take the steps necessary to achieve success. A contest with an unreasonable goal is much worse than no contest at all, for trust is undermined and participants begin to question the fairness of the entire compensation package.

Inclusive or exclusive

The next general principle: I must decide if the goal I have identified represents internal competition or if it sets a target, allowing as many as possible to earn the reward. Is it my intention to pit my team one against the others, or to set a benchmark, the attainment of which will result in some form of bonus? My experience tells me that either type of contest is equally effective when used exclusively, but the greatest positive impact comes when *both* are used in response to the occasion. There will be times when competition is needed, and there will be times when giving everyone a chance to "win" works best: a leader's job is to determine which makes the most sense, when.

Existing or new

Once I have determined the particular skills and/or activities to be rewarded in my efforts to help the team better attain the overall objective; decided on a goal that, while requiring extraordinary efforts, is still reasonably attainable; identified a definite means of measuring results; and determined the style of the incentive to be rewarded, I can move on to the next question. Am I trying to reward existing behavior, or do I provide sufficient incentive to actually change behavior? Providing an incentive for existing actions is usually easier and less expensive, making it the path that I am most likely to choose. However, there are circumstances when it is important enough to the business model for behavior to be changed altogether; under those circumstances the decision can be made to use a sales contest as the catalyst for those necessary changes.

If I do choose the latter approach, using a contest to launch an entirely new expectation, I must take additional time and perform in-depth analysis to determine which incentive would be necessary to incite the desired change. It is likely that I will discover that the level and the type of incentive needed to bring about an actual change in behavior will differ from one sales person to the next.

This added complexity and its associated costs are the primary reasons I would typically not use a sales contest as a means to change behavior. Each individual is motivated differently, and changing behavior requires motivation. Instead, to incite a behavioral change, I would be more inclined to create a coaching scenario with a defined goal and a reward associated with attainment—what would amount to an individualized contest within the context of one-on-one coaching. All that is to say, if I am going to design a contest with the idea of changing or introducing behavior, I must be prepared for greater cost, greater effort, and greater uncertainty of the outcome. If I include those probabilities in the design process, I can effectively avoid disappointment with the results.

One more thing, if in the back of my mind I am thinking that it is their "job" to change their actions, and that I should not *need* to provide additional rewards for them to embrace the new behavior, I risk resenting the team for my having to reward them. I will also most likely underestimate how significant the incentive must be in order to encourage the desired change and, as a result, I will create tension between the team and myself. Therefore, the decision to use a contest to change behavior, or any incentive for that matter, must be final and without resentment.

Time

When it comes to time, my experience tells me that within the framework of what I am trying to accomplish, shorter is better. If, for example, it is possible in a single day to properly emphasize the desired actions, then that is long enough. Whatever timeframe is necessary, whether a day, a week, or a month, structure the contest around those criteria and no longer. The key is *inciting desired behavior*. The quicker the incentive can be rewarded, the sooner the desired behavior can be recognized, and the more impact the incentive will have on the team. Running a campaign for a longer period of time than necessary has proved to be counter-productive in accomplishing the desired end result. On the other hand, running a campaign for too short a period may not allow for analysis of its effectiveness. These variances may demonstrate a need to use a little trial and error to become confident in the timing of a contest—that is perfectly legitimate. While you are testing, err on the side of brevity.

One last thought in regard to time. Not only is it important to run a campaign for a period of time no longer than that needed to incite the desired behavior, it is also important to space the frequency of your sales campaigns effectively. Obviously, when the purpose is to change or introduce behavior, the need will determine the frequency. For example, if you are rolling out a new product developed in response to market demand, its availability would determine the timing of any incentive designed to promote its introduction.

However, when the purpose is to add incentive for existing behavior, it is better to run fewer contests with greater rewards than constant contests with less significant benefits. To do the latter results in an inordinate amount of time and money being spent by your marketing department or by you in the process of designing campaigns and in developing the systems needed to track results; an inordinate expense that will not go unnoticed by your sales team. It is better to save the expense and increase the reward than to organize an entire department around designing less beneficial contests.

Reward

Which leaves only the logistics of actually delivering the incentive to your team. Setting the concept of significance aside, since that was covered above, the availability of the reward is very important. Sales persons find it discouraging to win a contest and yet have nothing to show for it but a promise that the "check is in the mail." Sales managers must make sure that whatever incentive was earned is available to be given to any and all rightful recipients as close to the end of the campaign as possible. There is a reason that the championship team receives the trophy immediately following their victory: they feel it more, which reinforces the actions that produced the win!

Most sales persons like to have the reward *tangibly* presented when they are recognized therefore, any additional planning needed to make sure that that can happen is worth the effort. Leaders should present the incentive itself, if it is tangible, or produce a certificate representing the incentive to be presented to the recipient if it is not. This may seem a minor thing, but my experience with hundreds of sales people proves its importance. Also, for most, but not all, sales persons, there is an added boost by having the presentation occur in front of their peers. Either way, in a group meeting or one-on-one, having a tangible awarding of the incentive is most desirable.

* * *

Designing an effective sales contest or campaign is very important in how it affects the budget, but even more so in how it impacts the sales team. There are enough campaigns and contests that have failed to produce the desired results (not to mention those that have actually become disincentives) to justify my taking a little more time and making the extra effort to do all I can to communicate the principles behind successful incentives. To that end, I have provided the following case study.

Case study

There is no activity that my sales team engages in that is more important than determining the need or needs of prospects and clients. Our company believes this enough to make it policy that every new prospect is interviewed to ensure that their needs are discovered. We also expect that existing clients with additional needs will have their profiles updated. Both new prospect and existing client profiles are supposed to be completed prior to any recommendations being made and a copy of each is automatically forwarded to me for review. Most of my team exceeds expectations in regards to the quality of the profiles they complete; those who don't are being coached and mentored. I would like to demonstrate to my team my appreciation for their efforts as well as reinforce the importance of accurately completed profiling forms.

As a tangible expression of my appreciation, I decide to design a campaign to reward profiling. I choose to narrow the focus, so the reward will be based solely on the number of new prospect profiles completed. Using the team average for new prospects seen each week and including the expectation that each prospect is profiled, I set the goal of my New Prospect Profiling Campaign: 10 new prospect profiles per week. That goal represents about a 20% increase above the current average, a bit of a stretch for my average and below average sales persons.

Since I already have a means of measuring the number of profiles completed (my standard business practice), I am already verifying the new prospect profile count, which ensures the accuracy of the count I receive during the campaign. And since I am actively involved in the day-to-day sales process, I can be confident that the profiles I receive will reflect real prospect interaction.

My primary purposes are to reinforce the current standard that my team members effectively profile each prospect and to show my appreciation for the importance of that activity. An ancillary benefit to using this particular activity is the possibility, though slight, that some of my team, who are struggling with their current number of appointments held, might focus additional attention on setting more appointments as a means to complete additional new prospect profiles and earn the incentive.

Because I want to highlight everyone's profiling efforts and, for my best profilers, to reward them for the exceptional job they are already doing, I set this goal as a benchmark and reward everyone who reaches it. Also, since I do not need to design an incentive of the magnitude needed to change or introduce new behavior, my expectation is that while rewarding existing behavior I will incite additional focus on the value of profiling during the time the contest is running.

The New Prospect Profiling Campaign I have designed will be a weekly campaign with rewards awarded on each ensuing Tuesday. I will run this campaign for six weeks—long enough to reinforce the importance of profiling, but not so long as to risk the focus becoming ineffective.

Since I had decided that the incentive would be for existing behavior, with a slight chance of changing behavior in some of my team members, I chose an incentive amount that represents between 5 – 10% of my team-average per sales person weekly income. I have found this ratio to be significant enough to encourage those who are new or struggling to focus on profiling—or any targeted activity for that matter—while still constituting a recognizable "thank you" for my top performers for their consistent, exceptional behavior. Since my sales team's average weekly income is $1500.00, I determine that the incentive will be $125 for each week the goal is achieved.

As mentioned above, the cash awards will be presented each Tuesday morning at the end of our weekly team meeting. I have made sure that I have adequate resources to award the incentive even if all eight sales persons on my team hit the benchmark each and every week. My budget for the campaign is $6,500.00, with $500 designated for expenses related to the campaign and the remaining $6,000.00 allocated for the awards themselves. This provides for an extremely efficient campaign with over 92% of the budget going directly to the sales staff. My expectation is that I will spend about 70% of my budget for this campaign.

After much time, research, and consultation with Ms. Smidget, you have decided on her compensation package as your new producing Sales Manager and the plan for your new sales team. She is quite pleased with her package and with the fact that you included her input in your design for her two sales people. Her opinion was that a plan that provided 60% of their total expected compensation in the form of salary and the remaining 40% through sales commissions and incentives would best create the environment of expertise for the clients and prospects. You liked that approach because after the training period it gave Ms. Gidgit and your son sufficient income, but would likely favor Ms. Gidgit with her industry knowledge and experience, providing your son with some peer pressure to incite him to catch up.

To enhance that variance, you also suggested a "fast start" campaign in which they both received extra incentive for each properly completed profiling form—properly completed meaning that not only was the information gathered but also that a solution was noted and justified. Ms. Smidget welcomed the suggestion for the benefits it would bring to her team's expertise in identifying needs and recognizing appropriate solutions and because it would help her to develop consistency in reviewing their profiling forms.

One last step before announcing the compensation package for the sales force was to have your new Sales Manager do some market and peer research to verify that the pay plan was going to continue to build your reputation as a great employer.

———○———

Compensation plans, including sales campaigns and contests, are the company's way of communicating what it values most. Good or bad, a company will attract the level of expertise and professionalism that its compensation package warrants. If you, as one of the leaders of your company, are dissatisfied with either the quantity or the quality of the effort being put out by your team, it *might* be that you don't have the right person for the job (how that might happen will be discussed in the next two chapters). Or, it might just be because the company decided it couldn't afford to design a compensation package that would attract better.

A Sales Manager is responsible to enable his or her team to develop expertise and to become the best they can; training, mentoring, and coaching are the primary means available to accomplish this development.

CHAPTER EIGHT
Team Development

This may seem a bit odd coming from someone who designs and delivers sales training, but training cannot do everything for your team. There are sales managers whom I know who overuse training, considering it the only means of bringing about change. And while *training* certainly has its place, it should be augmented and at times even replaced by *mentoring* and *coaching*. Competence (the state of possessing adequate knowledge and skill) can be trained, but expertise (the state of having specialized knowledge attained through experience) must be gained by practical experience, either one's own, or through someone else's via mentoring and coaching. Fortunately, you as a leader can use all three of these tools to help your team succeed.

Training is the conveyance of information in an organized and dedicated setting with the goal of improving skills and abilities. For our purposes, training is a cooperative effort between you and a designated trainer or trainers. (Though you as a sales manager can "train" members of your team, I include that as a part of the coaching tool described below.) Typically, training is most effective when specific skills such as product knowledge, sales skills, certain aspects of communication skills, interpersonal-relationship-building skills, paperwork processing, etc. need to be emphasized; when progress can be measured and monitored; and when direct impact is desired.

In the context of team development, mentoring is the sharing of professional experience and expertise by one member of the team with another (though leaders can "mentor" their team, the direct or indirect presence of performance standards moves me to refer to that as a part of the coaching process). Mentoring works best as a means of deepening a sales person's knowledge and experience, especially for the intangible or "soft" skills needed to be effective in such activities as interviewing, analyzing needs, the more artistic aspects of communication, and passing on expertise. Mentoring does not depend on setting goals or benchmarks, and is not an attempt to produce direct results, but rather influences someone toward change based on relationship and experience.

Coaching is a combination of training and mentoring principles as implemented by sales managers. Coaching is used for the direct purpose of bringing specific improvement to a team member's ability to identify and satisfy the needs of the consumers in the company's market. Coaching stands in between training and mentoring, providing leaders the opportunity to measure and assess the progress that is being made in a hands-on, one-on-one setting.

> For the last six months, you have been able to progressively give Ms. Smidget more of the Sales Manager's responsibilities until, after two years with Widget Enterprise she has assumed the role completely. Since you are the President of the company, she reports directly to you. She and your three other direct reports meet weekly to review progress on objectives and goals. Two months ago, she suggested that it would be good to bring on

two more sales people—your market share now stands at 25%, and each sales person has a 7% market share goal. By making these additions, she recommended, she can concentrate all of her time on her sales manager duties and turn her "book" over to the team. She also suggested that the sales training that was used six months ago would provide the new hires with the skills they need to be successful (and suggests that elements of it would be good refreshers for both of the current sales reps).

You accepted her recommendation, turning the hiring process over to her; asking only that you be given the opportunity to review her hiring interview after she writes it out and, to meet with the finalists to share your vision for the company to make sure that they understand the corporate philosophy as it relates to client satisfaction.

Over the last few weeks you have provided her with insights from your own recruiting and hiring experiences, let her borrow a book on recruiting, and had her spend some time with your Human Resources Manager to ensure that she was comfortable with all appropriate regulations in the hiring process. Recruiting took longer than she had anticipated, partly because one of her finalists ended up having a personal emergency take him out of contention thus requiring Ms. Smidget to interview a couple of other candidates for a third time to finalize her selection. But, last week, she was finally able to bring the two new sales people onboard under a training contract.

In today's meeting, Ms. Smidget asked for some help. The sales consulting and training company you use had originally been penciled in for the week before last week; assuming that that schedule would have allowed for sufficient time to find the two new candidates. Unfortunately, with the added time for recruitment and the consultant's existing commitments, it would now be three more weeks before the training company could be available to conduct the formal sales training for the new sales reps. Her request to you was to help her find an effective use of the next three weeks in preparing the new sales persons for success. You offered to consider it throughout the remainder of the day and scheduled a time with her mid-morning tomorrow to discuss your thoughts.

In most cases, to have the greatest positive impact on the team, leaders implement a combination of personnel development tools. It is up to leaders to determine when each of the available tools (training, mentoring and coaching) makes the most sense, but it is helpful to know that there are a variety of solutions to facilitate the need at hand. What follows is greater detail on how and when each tool can be effectively used.

Training

Training is like any other form of communication: the one with the idea must take responsibility for its transference to others. If it were just a matter of "saying" something, leaders could simply hand sales people a manual to read and save the cost of time and money that training would incur. But training is more than that. Training is used because it has been determined that something is lacking in the sales team's performance or that a new process, approach, or product must be introduced. Training represents the best way to ensure the successful implementation of those changes by utilizing a formal means of conveying the knowledge and skills needed.

Though it is technically possible to train one person, the nature of training indicates that it is most effective when used with a group, making it the best way to facilitate improvement for the team in its entirety. As mentioned above, training is designed and presented by a trainer either from within your firm or from an outside vendor. Training, as a tool of development, is used because it is believed that if the participants already *knew* what needed to be done to improve their performance, they would be doing it—they are the right people for the job after all—and because training allows for measurable accountability toward that improvement.

The effectiveness of training as a tool for team development depends on the cooperative, intentional implementation of all three aspects of the process. A good analogy that illustrates the training process is the swinging of a baseball bat, a golf club or even a tennis racquet. The swing begins with the **acceleration**, which leads to the actual **contact** with the ball, and ends with the **follow-through**—three separate and distinct phases, one swing. Proper training also has three separate and distinct phases: discovery and design, content delivery, and application. All three are vital; all three are interdependent; all three together determine the extent of the impact of the entire process.

There is however, a tendency to focus on only one of the phases: content delivery. This focus is partly the result of leaders who misunderstand how to effectively utilize training and therefore fail to embrace the importance of all three phases. The many off-the-shelf training programs that concentrate their efforts on the "contact" reinforce this tendency. Others pay some attention to the "acceleration" but have very little focus on the follow-through after content delivery. In baseball, a swing with only a little acceleration and no follow-through is called a bunt, and though a bunt may be appropriate at times, it should certainly not be the normal outcome of either a "trip to the plate" or of training. For your team to get the most out of the "swing," all three phases must be executed successfully.

Interestingly enough, there is an amazing parallel between good training and good sales: both require the effective identification and satisfaction of a need, and for both, the consumer determines satisfaction. In the sales process there is profiling, presenting, and promise delivery; in training there is discovery and design, content delivery, and application. In both processes, there is a tendency to concentrate on the "solution" and to pay less attention to the pre-work and follow-through; in both, the process is most successful when each phase is allowed to work synergistically with the others.

Discovery and Design
Effective training begins with a discovery phase. It is during this first phase that the consultant/trainer identifies the needs of your team and determines the needs that are within the trainer's area of expertise and that are a priority for you. The trainer then uses this insight to design a training solution that will satisfy your needs and priorities. When this "acceleration" phase is fully supported by you and given its proper attention by the consultant, momentum is created, participants begin to understand that what they are to be a part of has value, and prior training experiences—whether good or bad—are addressed to ensure proper expectations have been set.

A key to generating momentum for training is to have each attendee complete specifically designed and relevant exercises; exercises that not only help in the creation of the training solution, but that also prepare participants for receiving and applying the training content.

Those assignments intended to help in the formation of the content should include individual, specific interviews that give the attendees the opportunity to reflect on their own skills and weaknesses as well as on their experiences with and resulting attitudes from prior training programs. Properly designed, these exercises, like a well-designed profiling form, will help the participants recognize their needs as well as provide the consultant/trainer with vital information for constructing the solution.

Those exercises intended to prepare participants for getting the most out of the content should describe the training process itself, provide general expectations that the participants should have, and involve the sales team in the early stages of identifying results-driven activities—activities that when implemented will produce the desired improvements. These assignments are intended to prepare the participants for the behavioral changes that will need to take place if the purpose of the training is to be accomplished. They draw from the belief that the right people are in position, that they desire to be successful but need help discovering the means to that success. Though the training content will describe the means in detail, these exercises will help prepare the attendees so the content can have the greatest impact.

All of these assignments are geared toward creating energy and excitement about the benefits of the upcoming training sessions. When done properly, the pre-work will make the actual content relevant, pertinent, timely, and effective.

When you have committed to training as a means of team improvement, that commitment should be rewarded by results. Since the momentum or "bat speed" produces home runs, the pre-work before the training content is delivered must be the collaborative effort between the trainer and you to identify the training needs and to anticipate and accentuate the impact of the training solution.

Content Delivery

Once the need or needs have been identified and the training solution has been designed, the content itself should be delivered in a manner that allows the participants to "own" the information, to personalize and absorb it into their philosophies and practices. And though this is more difficult than it might sound, it is what you are paying for when you hire a trainer—someone who can help bring about an improvement in results, which implies bringing change at some level and degree to the sales process.

I do not intend to delve into the specifics of the adult learning model or the variety of means and styles that should be used by your trainers to facilitate the learning process. I do at least want to recognize that such details exist and must be attended to by those who train. Let it suffice to say that the end result of the "contact" phase should be the interactive determination of specific, measurable actions that the team members are to implement for the purpose of improving their ability to meet and exceed consumer expectations—what I refer to as agreed upon measurable goals or AMG's.

Application

With that as the goal for the delivery of content, it becomes only natural, if you want the training to "hit a homerun," for the training process to include accountability of and follow-through with the team in regards to those agreed upon measurable goals. The promise-delivery phase of a sale ensures client satisfaction and results in trust and loyalty for your sales persons. In a similar way, the application phase of training confirms the depth of the value that training brings to the development of your team and results in the confident employment of this tool when future needs arise.

If there is a lack of sufficient follow-through to the formal content delivery, whether because of misunderstanding of what makes training effective by trainers or by sales management or by both, there is a loss of some of the potential benefits that the trainings could have produced.

Trainers, both those within the firm as well as those from outside, should set the expectation upfront for follow-through. The best way to experience the change for which training was designed is to include a commitment to applying the principles trained and to following through with joint accountability to implement the agreed upon goals. As the one with the ideas that need to be transferred, the consultant/trainer is not only responsible for finding the "language" that the participants can receive, but also for developing the feedback mechanisms that can measure understanding. He or she must be willing to take accountability for the agreed-upon results *after* the content has been delivered. Sales management, for its part, must recognize that including and supporting the follow-through is the best way to ensure that the training is worth the price. The job is not done once the content has been delivered; the swing should not stop once the bat contacts the ball. Just as the follow-through propels the ball over the fence, so it is that post-contact accountability ensures that the desired results are actually experienced.

That is not to suggest that the trainer is to do the sales manager's job. Actions were identified during the pre-work and content delivery that will result in improvement for the team. The trainer should stay involved with the sales manager and the participants until it is clear that those actions have been understood *and* implemented. The follow-through phase produces the best results when done as a partnership between the consultant and the sales manager. This allows the on-site leader to carry the long-term accountability but provides the consultant as a catalyst in the early phases of change where momentum is most likely to be lost.

* * *

There will be times when a "training bunt" is appropriate and times when a quick refresher is needed or a very narrowly defined goal is acceptable. But bunts should be the exception, not the rule. As a leader, your decision to bring in a trainer to help develop your team is a serious consideration. The end results should justify the costs. Training is a tool for team development; by definition it is a formal process—meaning it takes time and commitment. The reason you choose to use training is that you believe it will produce the desired result—it will bring about the measurable change your team needs—and so it should!

Mentoring

When the development of your team is more a matter of the depth of expertise needed for the specific nuances of your industry or your market, mentoring represents a very realistic alternative or augmentation to the training process. Mentoring is certainly not a new concept. In fact, mentoring was the primary means of communicating expertise for the better part of human history, and was slowly replaced by training over the last 150 years or so. This evolution was due in part to the industrial revolution and the specifically tangible skills needed to perform manufacturing jobs. Is it any wonder then that as the U.S. economy becomes more and more "service" based, mentoring is again becoming more and more viable?

Evidence of the effectiveness of this sharing of experience and expertise can be found each time you look at one of the masterpieces of art and architecture throughout Europe, Asia, and even here in the United

States. The masters were mentored *and* mentors; they gained much of their skill from those who went before them and passed their expertise on to those coming after. History is filled with examples of mentor/ student relationships, many of the most famous demonstrating the greatest possible mentoring outcome: the pupil exceeding the master's skills.

Over the years, I have seen a few weak attempts at establishing true mentoring programs and even fewer occasions when its value was fully embraced, and I am honestly at a loss as to why. There are few or no hard costs attached to mentoring. Most sales people I know would be willing, even proud, to share their experiences. The benefits to all involved are noteworthy. The only conclusion I can draw is that leaders are either unfamiliar with how to implement a mentoring program, or they lack confidence in its effectiveness. I will address both of those issues beginning with the second of the two.

As to the effectiveness of a mentoring program for you and your team, much depends on the individuals who are a part of your team. If you have successfully recruited, hired, and retained quality sales people, mentoring is already happening. You will simply be lending it a forum and adding impact.

If, on the other hand, you question the quality of the expertise of some or all of the members of your team, for whatever reason, then expertise is not currently a commodity that can be exchanged among them: mentoring is not a realistic option. It would be best to first focus on the development of competence through coaching and training for those individuals, before including them in a mentoring program. Let me hasten to add that as is true with product/solutions, so it is with people. Perfection is not an option. There will not be a perfect employee to fill the role of a mentor. We are not trying to duplicate perfection. Rather, we want to share expertise.

For those with sufficient expertise, and as you develop the rest of your team to take on the role, mentoring can be exceptionally beneficial. Well-structured mentoring will become a dynamic means for you to reproduce the strengths of your team and reduce their weaknesses. Though it may be unrealistic to expect that mentoring will reproduce all the best of every sales person, and eliminate all the worst, it is certainly reasonable to anticipate a general improvement across the board as team members share their strengths with one another.

* * *

With an overall improvement and deepening of skills and abilities as the goal of your mentoring program, allow me to address the way to implement it effectively.

To begin with, leaders must believe that the team is made up of the right people for the job who are driven by the desire to be the best they can be. To be their best, competence is seldom enough; they need to develop expertise. And where training can bring them to the place of competence, their own experiences, mentoring by their peers, or coaching by their leaders can bring them to a place of expertise.

Once that belief is established, your efforts to install an effective mentoring program proceed by identifying each team member's strengths and weaknesses as they relate to the sales process. You can choose any of the following three ways to accomplish the assessment: 1) a self-assessment (although you may have had the members of your team do this previously, when you were recruiting or when you took on your role as leader, you may need to have them do it again to assure that your information is fresh and pertinent), 2) a peer-based assessment, or 3) a leadership assessment. I recommend using all three together. Take some time to review all assessments for consistencies and inconsistencies, with the goal of developing a single "sales person profile". This is unquestionably the most difficult part of the process, but not so hard as to make it an excuse for inaction.

Once you have developed the team's profiles, match each team member with strength in a given area to a counterpart with the corresponding weakness, focusing on only one characteristic at a time. For example, match a team member who is highly skilled at analyzing client information and identifying appropriate solutions with someone who struggles in that area. The variance in skill does not have to be vast for mentoring to work, but it does need to be recognizable.

Numbers may require you to match two-to-one, but normally it is best to keep it on a one-to-one basis. If you do it this way, each sales person is likely to be involved in two mentoring relationships: one in which the sales person is the expert and one in which he or she is the novice or non-expert. This approach also reminds all team members that they have something to give and something needed, which helps avoid anyone developing an unhealthy attitude.

Mentoring meetings should be a commitment, but by their very nature it is difficult for you as the sales manager to dictate when they are held. Allow each mentoring "team" to find the best time, place, and medium by which to meet—in-person or by phone (though the use of conference calls should only occur when vast geographic territories require it). You will want to monitor the consistency of the meetings as a part of your regular coaching activities to make sure that other priorities are not "squeezing" them out. Weekly meetings are a minimum, but due to your team's responsibilities they may also be the maximum. Part of what determines the frequency will be the length of time needed for the meetings to be effective: for a weekly schedule, I would suggest that at least thirty minutes be set aside. This gives enough time for the meeting to produce the desired impact without putting too much strain on the day.

You should also set a time frame for each mentoring team to stay in place; three months should be the minimum, six months may be better. It is likely that the person being mentored may not gain everything possible from his or her mentor in this time. It is preferable however, to cut the process a little short than to drag it on—it leaves them wanting more and creates excitement about the next round. Once the designated time has elapsed, take a look at each of the sales team members' profiles. Identify the next tier of strengths and weaknesses and reassign each of your sales persons to a new mentor.

After about a year—which would mean two to four mentoring cycles— complete a total reassessment of the team's skills and start again. By frequently reassessing and reassigning, you can prevent the process from becoming stale and provide opportunity for continuous improvement. By using this approach you also build in opportunity to insert any newly hired team members, after their initial training and integration period, into the mentoring program.

* * *

Under ordinary circumstances, everyone on the team will be enthusiastically involved in mentoring, being encouraged by the recognition of his or her own strengths as well as the opportunity to have his or her weaknesses offset in a non-threatening setting. However, unusual responses to mentoring may arise. Someone may lack enough strength in any of the primary skills and aptitudes needed to feel comfortable with mentoring a teammate; this often happens with a team you have inherited. When this is the case, I recommend that leaders, before including such a sales person in the program, take on his or her "mentoring" directly, making it a part of the re-fitting or coaching process (which we will discuss below). This saves the sales person from embarrassment and enables you to directly oversee his or her progress.

The other extreme reaction to establishing a mentoring program may be someone on the team refusing to take on the mentor role. He or she has the expertise to mentor but not the desire. Again, this is very rare, and I have only seen it in an inherited team setting. Never force a sales person to be a mentor. The sales person will either come around on his or her own and see the value to himself or herself and the team *or* prove himself or herself to be an unfit mentor after all.

* * *

Mentoring can have significant value and impact. It uses existing team members who possess offsetting skills as the resource to bolster strengths and minimize weaknesses for your sales persons precisely at their point of need. Mentoring is practical, providing personalized help for real problems. It not only gives real-world expertise to a struggling employee but also expertise that is specific to the very job he or she is trying to do right. Adding to this value is the sense a mentor has that he or she can make a positive difference, leading to an overall deeper loyalty to you and the team. Mentoring proves to be an extremely important resource to the company. If mentoring is fully embraced and done properly, almost every member of the team can mentor and be mentored. Most people have a strength they can share and a weakness they need to overcome. When you approach mentoring in this way, the synergistic benefits make it an ideal way to improve skills.

To some degree, mentoring happens without a sales manager's involvement. By choosing to proactively facilitate mentoring, leaders will ensure that the team experiences the benefits mentoring brings. In the end, the cost/benefit ratio of mentoring is extremely attractive. For little or no out-of-pocket expense, your entire team develops expertise. As you recognize the value of mentoring and find ways to activate and facilitate the mentoring dynamic, you multiply expertise exponentially, creating an environment where consumer satisfaction can become the standard.

Coaching

Coaching, which is a bit of a hybrid tool that leaders use quite often when developing specific team members, finishes off the three primary means you as a leader have in your goal to develop your team. Training is typically facilitated by an individual or team and delivered to measurably develop skills and aptitudes. Mentoring is the designed and focused interaction between peers with the purpose of communicating expertise from one to another in a non-goal-oriented environment. Coaching is the one-on-one interaction between the sales manager and a team member using training and mentoring techniques to significantly improve a team member's results. In some ways, by the very definition of leadership, your day-to-day involvement with your team is coaching. What I am referring to, however, is designated coaching sessions and activities designed for and motivated by specified behavioral changes.

Your company may already have a coaching format or process in place. The key for leaders to make the coaching process successful is to use a training approach, as described above, when there is a need to develop competence in a given skill set and to use the principles of mentoring when trying to develop a deeper level of expertise.

If there is a need for better listening skills, for example, as a coach you would "mentor" sales people by observing them in various settings and by allowing them to observe you. You would analyze their interactions and indicate areas needing improvement, and then provide skill development by modeling good listening skills and training the principles of effective listening.

Surrounding this would be specific listening assignments. One example would be to have them spend thirty minutes getting to know other team members by asking them specific questions and attentively listening to their responses. After the interview was over, they would write down what was remembered of the responses they heard. They would then give the interviewee the notes so that they could be checked for accuracy and understanding.

Your coaching would also have specific measurements for improvement in the designated behavior. Examples would be requiring them to complete a profiling form based on a pre-designed scenario so their effectiveness is accurately monitored, or requiring a specified level of improvement in their ability to recount product specifications after attending a training session, or some other measurable improvement specific to the areas in which they are struggling. The key is to help them get better—to provide them with specific tasks that will help them be better equipped to identify and satisfy consumer needs.

It is also vital that in setting goals for improvement the goal-setting methods we discussed previously be used. Identify specific markers that confirm that the sales person is developing the necessary skills. These markers, by which progress can be measured, should be fairly close together early in the coaching process to help bring hope and encouragement. Once your sales person has attained momentum, the measurements can and should be "further apart," requiring a greater level of competence and eventually expertise for them to be reached.

Be sure to keep a record of your coaching sessions. This is not only a good idea from a Human Resource perspective, but it will also help you as a leader to develop your own expertise, giving you insight into the patterns of development for the sales people in your industry and market.

> It is 10:30, time for your meeting with Ms. Smidget. You spent much of yesterday afternoon alternating between reviewing tax and accounting reports and mentally rehearsing your experiences as a manager, in sales as well as in general management roles. In considering the best use of time for the two newly hired sales reps, you concluded that they should use the first week to complete the Human Resources orientation, general product overview, and the assessments and interviews needed to prepare them for their upcoming sales training. They should spend the remaining two weeks being mentored. They could use the mornings to observe one of the two existing members of the sales force and the afternoons debriefing with Ms. Smidget on what they saw and learned, trading off every other day with whom they are partnered.
>
> After sharing your conclusions with Ms. Smidget, she lets you know that she likes the idea very much. Her only amendment is in regards to the mentoring schedule. She reasons that by remaining with the same sales person for the whole week the new reps will have the opportunity to become very familiar with one sales person's style. Then, when the switch occurs at the start of the third week, the differences in approaches will be emphasized—since both of the mentors are doing quite well, the lesson would be given that different styles work well

for different people, but the real key to success is putting the client's needs first.

You are impressed with her rationale and with how quickly you are able to move your attention from her "problem" back to the more taxing issues you are facing. Once again, you think about how glad you are that you took the time and effort to hire and retain expertise.

⟸◦⟹

Keeping in mind the primary objective of sales management (to enable and facilitate the delivery of the company's products and services to the consumers in a select market), having a sales team that is competent and in the process of developing expertise is one of the key means sales management has to fulfill that objective. Your team members were either hired by you—which means you had some input into their selection, or inherited—which means you did not. Whatever the case may be, they are a part of the team and thus should be looked upon as a valuable resource for your company's success. Developing them to be the best they can be will reflect on your value as a leader; helping *them* succeed will open doors of opportunity for *you* as a result.

You have at your disposal a number of tools that will help you develop your team: training, coaching, and mentoring are the three primary ones. Too often, whether by neglect or by accident, a sales person's development is left to self-determination. And though that may sound good, in reality it means that sales managers have missed out on the opportunity to experience the full advantages of having motivated, innovative individuals on the team.

When sales managers take a pro-active approach to team development, the team dynamic creates an atmosphere of continuous improvement. All the members of the sales force help to supply the need for energy, which is a constant demand for a sales organization. Clients recognize the high level of expertise and motivation and are thrilled with the superior treatment they are receiving. Your team achieves extraordinary success—success that rightly reflects on your leadership skills!

There will be times when it is determined that a sales person is not the right person for the job; being motivated by the consumer's best interest will encourage a Sales Manager to handle those circumstances with professionalism and grace.

CHAPTER NINE

Know When (and How) to Let Go

As a leader, your team was either built, inherited, or exists as a combination of the two; you were either a part of the selection and formation of all or some of the team, or you were not. In any event, the team is now yours to lead, in good times and in difficult times, the superstars and the benchwarmers. Chapter Three focused on how to build your team well through recruiting and hiring the right person for the job. This chapter will address the principles and skills you will need to determine that someone does not possess the competence and/or the desire to be the "right person" as well as how to proceed once you have made that determination.

> You find it hard to believe that it has been five years since you launched your dream, but next week marks the fifth anniversary of Widget Enterprise. You held your growth pace to just under 7% after your first year boom until you hit your original goal of 45% of the widget market about three months ago at which time you decided to buy out one of your competitors. Though not a "major" player, their facilities

were perfect for the inevitable expansion and modernization of production capacity you were determined to take on somewhere in the near term, and their 9% of the market would allow you to pay for the acquisition in about seven years—a very reasonable amortization. Personnel-wise, they ran a pretty lean shop. Those employees from the manufacturing side of the business will be interviewed to see if they have the skills needed to help in the minor conversion of facilities and processes and remain as part of the new facility. The office staff and officers were all members of the family ownership and will take their shares of the purchase price and move on. The sales staff consisted of two part-time employees, both of whom would like a chance to work for Widget Enterprise. As your Sales Manager, Ms. Smidget has agreed to interview each one and make a determination afterwards.

You hear a knock on your partly closed door, look up, and see Ms. Smidget standing in the doorway. You invite her to take a seat at your small conference table and step around your desk to join her. You reflect on her responsibilities as you take your seat: a total sales team of six full-time sales people, an assistant, and an intern. As you settle in, she jumps straight to the reason for taking up your time—she has interviewed both candidates and finds both to be adequately trained and reasonably coach-able. She tells you that during her interviews, both had mentioned their hopes, before the sale, of going full-time with their previous employer, each having their own life events that had recently precipitated their decisions. Before interviewing either one, she had actually anticipated how nicely two part-time sales reps would fit into the team—now she was faced with a bit of a dilemma.

Either might be a good addition, but she cannot justify bringing them both onboard. She understands that under the terms of the buyout, they will be entitled to a severance package if they were to be dismissed anytime from the date of the close of the sale until as much as six months later. Her question to you: would it be possible to bring them both on for a three-month training period and make a decision who would be the better fit after that time?

After briefly considering and asking a couple of clarifying questions, you let her know that you believe her plan to be good. There would be some additional costs associated with this approach, but in your mind, the importance of finding the right person outweighs those costs. You suggest that she treat them both as new employees, which will include the normal HR orientation, training, and mentoring programs; that she communicate verbally and in writing the terms of the training period; and that they spend the typical "first hour of their first day" with you to make sure they are exposed to your vision and business objective directly.

The reality is, since hiring the right person for the job is arguably the most difficult task a leader takes on, your predecessor may have struggled with his or her hiring practices. Therefore, it is possible, even probable, that you have members of your team who do not possess the proper skills, who never were told and/or grasped what was expected of them, and who have no real understanding of what leaders are there to do for them. Or, if you built the team, it may be that one of the people you recruited and hired has failed to live up to the standards of the job. Ultimately, as a sales manager, you may have to determine that either a good hire was not made in the first place or that the evolution of the job has been such that the expertise needed now is not a part of a particular team member's repertoire. Though not a particularly enjoyable part of your job, knowing when and how to let someone go is nonetheless an important skill for you to possess.

The circumstances that occasion the need to consider letting someone go fall into two major categories. Either you are coming in, as the new sales manager with existing team members who have been struggling *or* someone whom you originally hired has not met your expectations. I will look at both of these circumstances separately and then review your resolution options, since the skills you need to resolve either circumstance are the same.

Fear of the Unknown

If you are hired to take a leadership role for an existing team or if your company acquires an existing sales organization, you will be faced with some fairly unique and intense management challenges. People don't like change, even when it is an improvement. We all have a natural fear of the unknown—in this case, you, as the new leader, are the unknown! And that is true even if you were hired from among their ranks. If the prior leader's style was at least partially ineffective (a fairly safe assumption unless he or she was promoted within the organization you are joining), the team will be conditioned by ineffectiveness. It will take some time and experience for them to realize that you are not from the same mold.

During this transition you will face everything from skepticism and belligerence to flattery and insincerity. Your new team is confronting insecurity: their boss is gone, who will be next? Selling is a very competitive industry—there are opportunities for significant rewards, but that means there are equivalent risks as well. Those who have been successful may be concerned that you will limit their future opportunities in your attempt to equalize the playing field. Those who have been struggling . . . well they *know* what comes next. Your mission is to bring stability in the midst of change.

Along with the pressures from your sales team, you will want those to whom you report to see improvement. On very rare occasions, a sales manager is hired onto a well-performing team, with the expectation being that their performance is maintained—if you are offered a job like that, take it! Normally, senior management is looking to the new leader to provide measurable improvement "as soon as possible." You are up to the task, but to do it right, you will need to stay focused, and you will need to know your team, your market, your competition, and your unique opportunities. Though you most likely researched as much as you could of these components during your interviewing process, you are now in a place where you must make an in-depth, insider's analysis—starting with your team.

* * *

The initial step in the process of determining the fit-ness of your team is knowledge of the skills and aptitudes needed to do the job effectively. As the new leader, take some time to make sure you know what the job requires. Avoid making assumptions; instead, do appropriate research. Supplement what you learned in your pre-hire research by asking some of your internal peers and partners to describe what they believe it will take for members of your team to succeed. Contact some of your company's best clients and ask them for their input. Be thorough—your goal is to build a true, relevant job description that will help you lead your team.

Next comes identifying and assessing the individual strengths *and* weaknesses of each team member. (I say "next" but in reality these first two steps should be taken concurrently.) We discussed this in detail when we looked into the recruiting and hiring process; those same interviewing efforts should be made for everyone on your new team. I recommend that this be one of the first things you do when you enter a leadership position, rather than waiting for a problem to show itself. To do it right, you will need to take significant time and attention, which is why I suggest that you not wait until you have completed the "job" research noted above before you start assessing your team. You must know the need (the job that must be done), as well as the solution (the skills and expertise required of the sales person), if you hope to bring about the improvement desired.

Included in this step is the employee interview itself. If the job is complex enough, it may be helpful to provide a pre-interview questionnaire that gives you information about their more objective skills. Doing this allows you to focus on the sales person's personality and style during your face-to-face interview. If you haven't done so already, be sure to ask the sales team to assess their own strengths and weaknesses, prior to your individual meetings. This self-assessment will save you a significant amount of time and effort, but it should not replace your own assessment. Also, unlike interviewing for a new hire, you have the added advantage of a tangible record of performance and the strengths and weaknesses that that performance suggests. Use it, but do not rely on it exclusively. Each of these tools will give you insight into your team members and help you to develop your employee profile.

As a bit of an aside, you can expect this process to be somewhat threatening to the existing team members. Do what you can in how you present it to them to emphasize your true intentions: identifying and understanding their skill set in your efforts to help them be their best. From experience, I can tell you that, no matter how positively you present it, some of the sales team, especially those who have been struggling, will consider this the first step to their employment termination and will begin looking elsewhere. It is best—for you and for them—to proceed as if you did not know of that possibility. If they are not the right persons for the job and they move on of their own accord, then you are both better served. If, on the other hand, you find that they really do have the potential to be what your customers and clients need, you will be glad that you didn't allow yourself to be prejudiced against completing the assessment process.

Similar to the interview for a new hire, the interview for the existing team members must be well thought out. It should reiterate the essence and detail of the job to be done, focus on the skills needed to do that job right, and remind of or disclose the measurements that will be used to assess their effectiveness. The interview should also provide an opportunity for both parties to express sales person performance and managerial support expectations to determine if agreement exists. If agreement does not exist, there may have been a previous communication failure, which when corrected may result in a breakthrough.

Once you have completed the interview and you have used all the data gathered to create the sales person's profile, the hardest part of your evaluation is complete, but there is still work to be done.

As the new sales manager, you are expected to maintain stability for the team while finding ways to improve overall performance. While that can be accomplished effectively, it is not without great effort. Having the right people on the team is critical, but knowing whether the people are the problem or if something else is at fault requires a little more research.

The next question that needs answering relates to the sales person's understanding of the means of success. If the employee profile and its accompanying skill analysis points to the fact that the employee *should* be effective, you need to consider the possibility that he or she has been expending his or her efforts and talents on the wrong activities or in the wrong ways.

I alluded previously to the possibility that a breakdown in communication might be at the root of poor performance. For the sales person, the breakdown may be the result of a misunderstanding of his or her priorities or, a lack of appropriate feedback from his or her previous sales manager. Whatever the cause, making sure that the sales person fully understands what skills, talents, and actions are needed to succeed and giving him or her the opportunity to put those things into practice are quite often relatively inexpensive—by time and resource standards. With new or renewed insight into how to succeed, he or she just might.

The other possible explanation for concluding that the sales person has what it takes to succeed, even though he or she is not, would be the lack of true opportunity in his or her assigned territory. If you were not able to access a full analysis of your market demographics and the proxies or measurements used to allocate territories before being hired, you need to do so before making any personnel decisions. Just because your predecessor created or maintained the territories does not make their opportunity sufficient—it may in fact indicate why they might not be. Again, avoid making assumptions; analyze for yourself if true opportunity exists for your struggling employees.

You may determine that you have more sales people than your region can support. If that is the case, be prepared to provide a thorough explanation of why and how you came to that conclusion. Most senior managers are quite hesitant to reduce the size of their sales staff, but there will be times when it is in everyone's best interest to do just that.

On the other hand, you may determine that your region has enough opportunity for the number of sales persons currently in place, but the individual territories are not "sized" effectively. As you might remember, it is just this result about which some of your team may be concerned. It may be that there are those on your new team who have been exceptionally successful not because they are exceptionally talented, but because they have an inordinate opportunity. If this is the case, you will need to decide whether to rearrange territories to provide equal opportunity for each of your sales persons or to continue to favor some in an attempt to maintain stability. Unfortunately, this is not an exact science; you will need to use your best judgment. I can make a case for either approach, but without knowing the dynamics of the team, any advice I might give here would be too theoretical.

As with all management decisions, it often comes down to your personal philosophy. As long as you are consistent in how you manage your territories, it will work. However, when your team experiences inconsistency, hypocrisy, or a lack of integrity in your approach, you lose your ability to lead. If you are true to your philosophy, if you are preaching what you practice, then your leadership is intact.

* * *

As the result of your assessment of your new team you discover three probable causes of a sales person's ineffectiveness. The skills and opportunity are there, but they have been misappropriated. The skills have been applied effectively, but the opportunity is insufficient. The opportunity is sufficient, but the sales person does not appear to have the skills needed to take advantage of it. In all cases, you are committed to bringing about an improvement in sales and to leading your team to success.

A "Bad Hire"

The other situation that leads to needing to let a sales person go arises from what some refer to as a bad hire, though it might also be the result of an evolving job description and a static skill set. Ultimately, it presents itself when you have an individual hired by you who is not meeting expectations although he or she has sufficient opportunity to succeed.

You know you have communicated your expectations clearly, the sales person's behavior suggests that he or she understood what you expected, but the sales person is not meeting the goal. Because you hired the person and have managed him or her for a sufficient period of time, you know the person's strengths and weaknesses. Also, you have been an active part of his or her career development through observation and coaching, and you have provided regular opportunities for the sales person to enhance his or her skills. Despite all of this, the person is failing, and you need to do something about it.

Before you move too quickly, let me suggest that you consider updating your job analysis and individual skill assessments. With the dynamic nature of markets and consumer demands, the need may have changed, but the "solution" has not kept pace. In other words, your sales person has the skills that were needed previously, but the job requires new skills for today. To be successful your sales person merely needs to have his or her skills "upgraded"—which is a much better remedy than having to replace him or her completely.

> Sometimes the decisions we make that have the biggest impact are the ones that seemed almost insignificant at the time we made them. Seventy-five days ago, you agreed with Ms. Smidget's plan to bring both of the part-time sales persons from the competitor you purchased onto the team under three-month training

contracts. They participated in the standard new-hire training process, and according to Ms. Smidget's last report, both have been performing quite well. In fact, the greatest concern she had expressed was how she was going to choose whom she would need to let go at the end of the ninety days.

At least that was her greatest concern four weeks ago—then something quite unexpected happened. Ms. Gidgit, one of your first hires to the sales team, seemed to lose interest in doing the activities needed to successfully meet her clients' expectations, and the clients had noticed! After the first complaint came in, Ms. Smidget met with Ms. Gidgit to discuss what had occurred. The response was not what Ms. Smidget had expected: not only was Ms Gidgit unwilling to take responsibility, but she showed extreme resentment at being questioned. It was hard to imagine that things could go from good to bad so quickly, so Ms. Smidget initiated some quality review assessments with some of Ms. Gidgit's other clients. (You had realized after the weekly meeting in which you first learned of the situation that previously you had felt no need to implement a system of quality controls on the sales side—although they were commonplace on the manufacturing side of your business. This realization caused you to jot a quick reminder note to yourself to instigate a full review of your sales standards and practices with Ms. Smidget before the start of the next quarter.)

The last three weeks included some very shocking revelations: much of Ms. Gidgit's business had been repeat orders from long-time clients who were "low maintenance" accounts, those clients who *had* required direct service from her expressed great dissatisfaction with her responsiveness, and her personal referral numbers and her activity numbers were slightly above average for the team, but could not be validated. In response, Ms. Smidget instituted an intense refitting strategy about twelve days ago that included daily coaching sessions, access to outside counseling (in case Ms. Gidgit's work issues were related to a personal crisis of some kind), the opportunity to participate in additional mentoring sessions above and beyond the normal program, and nearly twenty-four/seven access for whatever help that might be needed. Despite all of these efforts and for no discernable reason, there continued to be no indication from Ms. Gidgit that she was interested in improving. Based on her lack of motivation, the growing complaint file, and her impact on the overall morale of the team, Ms. Smidget placed Ms. Gidgit on a third-level improvement plan and gave her until the end of the month to turn her attitude and performance around.

Everyone on the management team supported the decision. They were all a little shocked as well. For the first time in the more than five-year history of Widget Enterprise, it appeared that someone's employment would need to be terminated. Sure, there had been people who had chosen to leave, but always before it had been on good or at least amicable terms. But the need to provide clients with the expertise and satisfaction they required was too important to the health and reputation of the company to not take strong action. If after every attempt to fix the problem had proven futile, then letting Ms. Gidgit go would be the right course of action for everyone on the team. And though you, Ms. Smidget, and the rest of your management team understood that to be true, it did not make the fact any easier to accept.

Re-fit or Release

When, after leaders have done a thorough review of the job, a detailed skill assessment, a full analysis of opportunity, and a complete communication of expectations and confirmation of understanding, and have come to the conclusion that a team member is ill equipped to do the job he or she is required to do in the way it should be done, what do leaders do? Whether what precipitated the realization was your taking on the leadership role of an existing sales team or the underperformance of someone who was hired by you, you have a choice to make. When it is clear that you have a member of your team who is unable or unwilling to effectively and adequately identify and satisfy consumer needs you are left with two options: you can either attempt to develop that person into a solid, performing member of the sales team, or you can let that person go.

Under all but the most extreme circumstances, I recommend that you develop an action plan with the ultimate goal of bringing the employee's skills up to standard. As with any good goal, it should be measurable, time-bound, and reasonably attainable. This action plan must be founded on a clear communication of expectations, thereby removing any misunderstandings and correcting any misdirected efforts that may have contributed to the sales person's prior poor performance. Knowing a sales person's weaknesses focuses your time and attention on those areas vital for the re-fitting process—giving your action plan clarity. Knowing a sales person's strengths gives you something for which to praise the employee, producing opportunity for hope and encouragement—catalysts for change. The action plan would include the use of the tool, or combination of tools, that you determine to have the greatest likelihood of successfully turning the sales person's career around.

Every effort is being made to change the leopard's spots, so to speak—and you may be asking, why? Why the extreme amount of effort for the sake of an employee who is presently considered unable to do the job right?

Why?

Have you considered the alternative?

The effort and expense needed to recruit, hire, train, and equip a replacement, as well as all the risk and danger incumbent with it, are what you will otherwise be faced with. Since you know the objective of the job and that the core opportunity is sufficient, the skills needed for success are identified, and the skills possessed have been assessed, your ability to determine your chances of facilitating the required change is fairly strong. My experience tells me that you are much more likely to convert a benchwarmer into a solid member of the team than you are to hire a "superstar" off the street or from your competition.

Those sales people looking for work are probably only adequate performers; those you might "win over" show a lack of loyalty that can inevitably be as detrimental to you as it would prove to be for their current employers. There are relatively few circumstances when superior sales persons are available. However, as you develop the reputation of being the kind of employer who rewards expertise, you will know when those circumstances exist and will be able to take advantage of them. But, normally, the better approach is to develop your sales team, not attempt to "buy" it.

With your current "leopard," you know what you have, you have assessed his or her strengths and weaknesses, you have a good idea what resources are likely to be expended in an attempt to change his or her "spots," and you know your likelihood of success. With someone new, you have only the unknown to depend upon.

All in all, my best advice is to examine the employee's desire and motivation levels. If the person is willing to put out the effort to make a change, it is usually a good investment of your time and energy to give him or her that opportunity.

* * *

And though it is my position that normally leaders should put out the effort to re-train and equip, I do understand that there will be times when, despite your best efforts or because of the employee's lack of drive, it is in everyone's best interest to let an employee go.

In all possible evaluations, leaders have two real options: re-fit or release. In those scenarios and assessments where re-fitting does not make sense, leaders must move the team forward.

When your best efforts prove to be futile, when it is discovered that a sales person is incapable of doing the job the way it needs to be done, you must believe that helping to identify which skills and aptitudes the employee *does* possess—or at the very least, those which they clearly do not possess—will give the employee the greatest opportunity to find his or her "right job" somewhere else. Helping them to enter into a career in which they truly believe may be a greater service than anyone else has ever provided to them.

Grace and kindness should be used at all times, which often includes not prolonging the agony of the inevitable. Complying with your company's HR practices will provide you with all of the legal and official forms and format, but keeping the best interest of your customers and clients in mind will help you proceed with determination and empathy. Being confident in the value consumers place on expertise and recognizing your role in making sure they have access to it will help you stay true to the principles of leadership—for everyone's sake.

―――◦――

The skills and steps taken to evaluate existing employees are quite similar to those used to recruit and hire the right people in the first place. As a leader, you will face situations that require an assessment to be made, when a person's career will be affected by the outcome. This is a serious part of your job, one that no good sales manager ever takes lightly.

Due to the gravity of personnel decisions, time and consideration must be taken to evaluate all aspects of the job. As a leader you need to be confident in the sufficiency of the opportunity, aware of the skills needed to succeed, knowledgeable in regards to the sales person's strengths and weaknesses, and familiar with their level of desire and motivation. From that position you are able to effectively assess what actions are in your employee's, your company's, and, most importantly, your customers' and clients' best interests. If it is determined that the employee's desire and motivation to succeed warrants the effort to re-fit them to the job, you have the tools needed to do so successfully.

When, however, they are either unwilling or unable to change, addressing the situation in a straightforward and direct manner is always best.

There are regulations that govern your process, but in all cases your professionalism and true leadership will enable you to make the best of even this most difficult situation.

Section Two
The Philosophy of a Leader

CHAPTER TEN

Extraordinary

"You are all leaders."

That was what the new president of our division had said. "All" meaning the 350 or so in attendance, some of whom were justifiably concerned that the merger would mean the end of their career with the company.

It was a typical annual sales meeting for a large regional bank's investment department—with this one added import: our parent company's solution to a hostile takeover attempt had resulted in a "friendly merger" with another west coast bank holding company, a company that just weeks earlier had been one of our chief rivals. It was at these meetings that we all hoped our direction and destiny with the new firm would be revealed—or at the least hinted at.

I sat in a section of the large conference hall near many of my team members. As their sales manager, they were looking to me for assurance that any changes to come would be good… and that they would be around to enjoy them. I gave my team what reassurances I could: we had been one of the top regions in the company, our average production was well above the average production of the firm as a whole, and they were RPU's (revenue producing units) which were always looked upon favorably by management—especially after a merger.

As for me, it was my second "tour of duty" as a sales manager, and though I had received no formal leadership training, I had experienced a great deal of success; turning a previously mediocre territory into one of the top three in the Pacific NW. I had recruited and hired successfully, done a good job turning my below-average performers into solid producers, and had helped a couple of misplaced sales people move on to more suitable careers. But, I could not shake the phrase 'to the victor go the spoils' from my mind.

These were my thoughts as I engaged in small talk with those around me; my own attempts to provide for myself the same reassurance, the same sense of confidence in my value that my team was seeking.

It was while contemplating these thoughts and trying to analyze for my team and myself the likely implications of our merger that our new boss began to deliver his message. Looking out at the sea of faces—obviously aware of our anxiety—he opened with the only line of his speech that I still remember: "I want you to know that I believe you are all leaders!"

"… you are all leaders."

Maybe it was the poor acoustics, but that phrase seemed to echo around the room—"…you are all leaders."

I couldn't help it, there was something not quite right, something off kilter with that statement—the analytical side of me took off at full throttle. "You are all leaders?" I asked myself, then why have my team and I been working so hard to improve? "You are all leaders" the phrase resounded in my mind. How could that even be possible? Doesn't the very concept of "leader" require a separation from the crowd? As he continued his speech I tried to picture some 350 people all crossing the finish line at the same time—the scene in my mind was so ludicrous I nearly chuckled aloud. "All leaders," why would he even say such a thing? He must define that word differently than I do.

Everyone knows the competitive nature of sales people; surely he was not suggesting that both good and bad results were equally acceptable.

No, I decided, it must be an attempt to stabilize the sales force, to assuage concerns so that everyone would continue to give their best efforts, or at least not jump ship, while upper management sorted out the implications of overlap and duplication. Common sense—etymology itself—points out the impossibility of the idea: "you are all leaders."

And so on, and so on went my thoughts until my reverie was broken by the polite applause of the crowd, the kind of applause that suggested that there had been a great deal more questions wanting to be asked than there had been answers given.

But that one phrase, "you are all leaders," would have a dramatic impact on my career. Much more dramatic than the implications of this or the two other mergers I would later endure. Though I eventually decided I couldn't support the direction the new firm wanted me to take my team, I left it personally richer because of what that phrase had begun to work in me. I had come to a defining moment in my own development: it was the definition of "leader" and it would take me in a whole new direction!

Sales Manager—Leader
Leaders are extraordinary people.

Ordinary meaning usual or customary: extraordinary meaning very unusual and deserving attention for being excellent; having a special purpose.

By definition, leaders are those who are in the forefront, those who face the greatest resistance, those who set the pace and who provide an example for others to follow. Leaders are those most likely to be praised for their accomplishments—and criticized for failures. True leaders are followed willingly, not because of title or position. And the best leaders not only know their followers, but care about their welfare.

Leaders can be found throughout history, though sometimes *only* from the perspective history provides. There are leaders in every arena, profession, discipline and aspect of life. Mothers, fathers, doctors, diplomats, philosophers, generals, athletes, executives, educators, students; every race, society, class, nation, ethnicity; every age, time and moment has its leaders. Leaders are those who rise up to meet the needs of their time and who find a way to do what the circumstances require. Some, like Winston Churchill were almost overlooked; others such as President Kennedy possessed such charisma that they seemed pre-destined for their roles. There are leaders like General "Vinegar Joe" Stilwell, known as leaders of the people and there are leaders like General Patton, who are not. Among all of their differences, leaders have one distinction in common—they *are* extraordinary.

This book was written for sales managers because sales managers are in position to be leaders—that means that your leadership is not automatic, but it is greatly needed. You have the opportunity for excellence and a special purpose.

Recognizing the leadership responsibilities of your role can be somewhat intimidating. Sales managers with whom I speak are often comfortable with the operational and logistical roles they are required to fill, but balk at their role as leaders. I understand this hesitance.

Despite the cliché, leaders are made not born. Certainly there are some who have an easier time leading than others, but all who lead must develop the skills necessary to do so effectively. Yet it is extremely rare for a business to provide its management with any real leadership training.

* * *

Like most of you, I never received any formal training to help me develop and fulfill my leadership role as a sales manager, and so I have had to look to my peers and mentors as well as to leaders from history for inspiration, direction, and guidance. To that end, I have had the extremely good fortune of knowing some wonderful leaders who were willing to help me as my career developed. Much of what was expressed in the first section of this book is the direct or indirect result of those leaders; individuals who have taken an active role in my life and aided me in discovering the principles that enable a sales manager to succeed.

I have also looked back to history for extraordinary examples of leadership, for those who stood out in their day for their willingness to go beyond the ordinary. One such historical leader—though he is almost more mythical than real—is William Wallace. I remember reading *The Scottish Chiefs* by Jane Porter when I was just embarking on my sales career, providing me with an introduction to Wallace's character. And though it is semi-fictional, the movie *Braveheart* continued to spur my interest in William Wallace's impact on his people. So intrigued was I by his leadership; the dedication and devotion Wallace had for his people and their cause that I made a special trip, while in London on business, to visit Sterling, Scotland to see for myself the place of his greatest victory. From all that I have learned of Wallace, I have pieced together a portrait of a true leader whose example encourages and inspires me.

What made Wallace extraordinary, an inspiration of leadership, was his dedication to his people and their cause and his willingness to pay the price that that dedication would require. He was not looking for personal glory; he was looking to make life better for others. He knew what needed to be done, why it must be done, and the price that would have to be paid to do it. He knew he was willing to pay that price, as were those who stood with him. He believed that a small band of free men could defeat the larger armies of a tyrant—for he knew the power of freedom. He knew the importance of passion and hope to the heart and soul of those who fought beside him. And he *knew* that even if he didn't see the good that would result from their efforts, the good would come nonetheless.

As I have contemplated Wallace's life I have recognized principles of leadership, principles that don't change *wherever* and *whenever* a leader is needed. It is my goal in these next chapters, without over-reaching the parallels, to do all I can to impress you with the importance of what you, as a leader, can accomplish for your company, for your team, and for yourself.

* * *

In a competitive, free-market society such as ours, those from whom we, as consumers, buy goods and services directly impact the quality of our lives. We all know the sense of satisfaction that comes when a business meets our needs and exceeds our expectations, and the sense of frustration and disappointment when they do not. We have preferences and those preferences provide opportunities for businesses to succeed… or fail. We want to have our needs, goals and dreams fulfilled; products and services are designed and offered by companies to help meet those goals and dreams; sales people match their products and services to those goals; and sales managers are responsible to make sure that that sale is done right.

As a sales manager, your ability to effectively lead your sales team not only makes a difference for your clients and customers, but for your entire organization: clients' needs are satisfied and you, your team, and your company succeed!

* * *

Leaders can accomplish greatness by effectively influencing others in the decision to be their best. Leaders need to not only do the hard things; they need to effectively do the hard things the right way. Leaders are important in any field or occupation: politics or poetry, theater or theology, science or sports, education or enterprise, defense or diplomacy.

Leaders do not focus on efficiencies alone, but on end results. Yet true leaders, in their pursuit of results, do not justify the means by the ends. True leaders understand that no lasting success comes through doing wrong.

Leaders are valuable, extremely valuable, which is to say that they have great utility and relative rarity—great utility because they facilitate the accomplishment of those things that need doing; relative rarity because of the high price exacted on those who choose to lead.

If leading were easy, anyone could do it, but no one would need it. The nature, the very definition, of leadership suggests a willingness to take a path that ordinary people would not choose.

Leaders are not concerned with titles or positions but with cause and purpose. Great leaders of the past and present are those individuals who develop the ability to determine the right course of action *and* the capacity to inspire others to follow them in it. Where the ordinary person can possess a certain degree of satisfaction knowing what needs to be done and how to do it, leaders understand that the reasons for doing, the motivations for acting, are sometimes even more important than the doing itself.

In the case of William Wallace, his motivation was grand and good; it reached beyond himself and reflected the needs of his fellow Scots. His motivation, being "good," enabled him to inspire others to greatness. The worthiness of his endeavor empowered those who followed him to do greater things than they could ever have done if their own interests drove them alone. William Wallace knew *why* he had to do what he did, and that conviction helped him to find the means to do it.

* * *

There are many extraordinary characteristics of the leaders I have known and read about, but the two that stand out most are vision—the ability to clearly see the path that must be taken—and passion—the drive to take that path despite opposition and risk. Make no mistake, when leadership is required, there will be opposition and risk—otherwise ordinary would suffice.

Think about the most outstanding leader in your life, the person from whom you draw your greatest inspiration. I am sure that even a cursory look at his or her life and exploits would reveal an individual of great vision and passion, someone who lived or is living a truly extraordinary life.

William Wallace was a leader who was confident in his vision and purpose; this confidence gave him the courage to attempt the "impossible." Though under-trained and under-equipped, he and his men would risk their lives to free the people of Scotland from the grasps of one of the greatest powers of their age.

You too might be under-trained and under-equipped. Though you are not faced with the same mission as Wallace, having a vision and passion for the significance of the mission you do have can encourage you and your team to also attempt the impossible. There will be times when you will need to push through resistance and overcome obstacles to help your team succeed. You will need to exemplify the actions and attitudes that perpetuate success, and provide direction and guidance to those you are leading so that they, too, may be able to participate in the thrills of achievement. You will be required to measure the risks, weigh the alternatives, and count the costs—and then act—for you are their leader!

It is one thing to see what needs to be done and yet not have the drive or motivation to do it; it is quite another to have the insight to discern *and* the passion to act: having both defines a leader. And though the scale of significance as compared to the exploits of your hero may *seem* to suggest otherwise, in truth this ability to discern and willingness to accomplish are equally important to leaders in all realms... including yours.

I am not attempting, through my comparisons, to overstate the importance of Sales Management. But as I see it, greatness is much less about the *scope* of one's impact than about the *scale*. You or I may never be asked to lead the fight for our nation's freedom from tyranny, but that does not mean that we should misjudge the importance of the leadership we can provide in the places in which we work, the places we will spend nearly 50% of our waking hours. To give our best within the realms and spheres of influence in which we live *is* leadership, please don't underestimate its importance.

* * *

No worthwhile business endeavor has ever been undertaken without a vision, the ability to see a need that remained unfulfilled. Leaders recognize the need; leaders discover the means of satisfying the need; and leaders transfer the vision to others, so that they might participate in the business's success.

The average employee will spend somewhere in the neighborhood of 100,000 hours working to build his or her career—for most, being a part of something beyond the ordinary is a much more desirable use of that time. When hoping to build a career with a successful business, employees will naturally look to a leader to reveal the corporate vision—the reason the company exists, the path it has chosen to take.

Most employees I have met want to excel; none have confessed a yearning to be mediocre. For excellence to happen, they need a leader to provide an understanding of and passion for what drives the company. If they are going to succeed in their various roles and responsibilities, they must know more than just how to do their jobs; they need to understand "why" they should do their jobs exceptionally. They need the heartfelt expression, by leadership, of the foundational principles upon which the business was and is being built—the communication of that vision is key to bringing out people's best.

The impartation of vision translates into extraordinary efforts and extraordinary results from ordinary people; leaders inspire us, and we respond with our best. Successful businesses must have a leader with vision and passion and the ability to convey those qualities, a leader who by understanding the hearts of the employees is able to influence them to produce great things.

Leadership in a business environment is what produces innovation, invention, and entrepreneurship, whether for the entire company or for a single department. In a leader's unwavering knowledge of the business's mission and objective are life and passion. In his or her ability to clearly see the means of accomplishing that mission is the path of success. It is the communication of that vision and passion that draws the rest of the team into the pursuit of excellence.

If vision and passion are vital to employees in general, they are even more so for those in sales—as a sales manager you already know this to be the case. Within the overall business model, the sales team's specific purpose is the distribution of the company's solutions (products and services) to consumers. As you enable and facilitate this distribution, communicating the vision or mission of the employer to the sales team is imperative. It is also vital that you communicate to the team *their* importance in accomplishing the mission. And that is true whether your team is made up of one or one million members; it is the cumulative, impassioned effort of the entire sales team that brings about success.

Knowing and understanding your company's mission and believing in each employee's role in accomplishing that mission provides an atmosphere for extraordinary employee involvement, and gives them reason to be motivated to the exceptional.

Leaders are vital, they provide the direction, guidance and inspiration required to accomplish the extraordinary. They are looked upon as examples, expected to overcome any and all obstacles, and relied on for the successful completion of any worthwhile endeavor. Leaders also are the source of vision and passion—the ability to discern and the drive to choose the right course. The need for leaders is great and that need exists in all areas of life… including in the realms of business.

Incorporated in your role and your responsibilities as a sales manager, is that of "leader." As a leader, you are responsible for expressing vision to your team. Therefore, you *must* have your company's vision clearly imprinted in your mind so that you can communicate it. Since it is vision that directs a company and the impassioned efforts of all employees that enable it to succeed, ensuring that all of your sales people clearly understand and are driven by the corporate mission is critical. If your sales team is clear about their direction, their efforts are focused, their passion is harnessed, and their results are extraordinary.

CHAPTER ELEVEN
Cause and Effect

Businesses are not started by accident—their founders had a vibrant vision and a driving passion; the challenges of business ownership are far too great for it to be otherwise. There was, and at some level must still be a reason for being, a primary motivator. And though it may seem theoretical, ensuring that employees understand and "buy into" a company's cause is extremely practical: it encourages employees to give their best. Leaders must make sure that any gap between what birthed and drives a business and the typical employee's understanding of the company's purpose is bridged.

Do you know your company's vision? Have you been told or are you aware of why the company you work for was founded and why it continues to exist? How about the rest of your team? How much do they know about the "why" behind your business's objective? Employees want the companies for which they work to be successful; knowing what lies behind a business can motivate them to be extraordinary because it opens their eyes to the grander scheme.

So, just how important is the cause and drive behind a business's existence?

Though all businesses want to be successful, not all are. In my experience, it is the motive, the *primum causa*, behind the start of a business that determines its chances for success. An effective indicator of what will *make* a business successful and what will *keep* a business successful can be found in its reason for being.

Here is what I mean. A business can typically be launched from one of two platforms. The first is the entrepreneur seeing an opportunity and believing he or she can **capitalize** on it. The motive of this approach is therefore profit-centered. The second is the entrepreneur seeing a need and believing he or she can **satisfy** that need more effectively than those businesses currently attempting to do so. The motivation here is to provide innovative consumer satisfaction.

The issue is not whether or not to be successful—every business hopes to be successful; the issue is identifying and persisting in the means for being so. A business can either make profitability its cause *or* the consequence of doing business in a way that is satisfying to the market. Though this difference in motivation may seem insignificant, even trivial, in reality it is the most important aspect of any business model— it is the "why" that leads to the effective answer to every other question that may arise in the business's history.

Focusing on the ability to be profitable puts the cart before the horse. Lasting profitability is the *effect* of doing business the right way; it is what happens when a business does a better job of developing loyalty, through successfully satisfying the consumer more consistently than its competition. Leaders understand this difference, live by it, and pass it on to the rest of the team. Success is always the desired end; leadership is the catalyst for achieving that end.

Said another way: businesses exist to satisfy the legitimate needs of the consuming public. Successful businesses are those that are led and managed by individuals who possess a passion and vision for why their business exists; a detailed and practical knowledge of their markets, their competition, their strengths, and their weaknesses; and who then use that knowledge to effectively satisfy the needs they have identified, thereby earning the trust and loyalty of their customers and clients, as evidenced by repeat business and personal recommendations.

The Business Model

The primary purpose or cause of any business is to innovatively satisfy a consumer-based need within the business's chosen market. The business "plan" then consists of specific strategies that, when implemented well, lead to the proficient use of the assets and resources at the business's disposal while minimizing any liabilities or deficiencies. The implementation of these strategies by leadership results in the day-to-day operations of the business: the specific tactics the business will use, the activities in which it will engage. Success is realized here, in the effective execution of strategies.

Again, any business in a relatively free market economy exists to meet a need or needs. Markets change, costs of doing business change, resource availability changes, and any business, in its daily operation, must take these changes into account and respond accordingly. However, the cause, the purpose, the primary objective should not change and, by definition, *cannot* change.

Here's an observation that may help make my point: of my six sons, five are playing or have played football (the sixth, just seven years old, is likely to follow suit), and throughout my many years of observing the game, one thing is clear: at all levels, from Optimist or Pop Warner to Junior and Senior High to College to every manifestation of professional football, the objective of the game does not change. The overriding goal is always to have more points than your opponent at the end of the allotted playing time.

The game implements two major strategies: offense—getting the ball into your opponent's goal as often as possible and in compliance with the rules of the game; and defense—legally preventing your opponent from getting the ball into your goal. Those two strategies are performed through individual plays, which are simply the allocation of assets and resources in such a way as to effectively accomplish the objective. The coaching staff (which would align with the leaders of a business) must design a wide variety of plays that bring about success, plays that highlight a team's strengths and cover over the team's weaknesses. Good coaches make adjustments throughout the game as new strengths are presented and new weaknesses are exposed. Though it might be very *efficient* for the coaches to have the team run the exact same play over and over again, on offense and defense, it would not be very *effective*; it would not produce success, the team would not achieve its primary objective.

And so it is in every business; the objective or cause remains the same—strategies are overriding, but the day-to-day operations must be dynamic. A business must constantly analyze its environment, ready to change the means by which the business attains its goal in response to its markets. If a client wants a different solution, when technology improves, as markets adjust, the business must be able to "change the play" in response. In their efforts to respond to these changes, leaders must not just know their team's strengths and weaknesses, leaders must account for them in the daily operations, designing "plays" that maximize the positives and minimize the negatives.

In business, change is inevitable. Having been given the responsibility to lead, you must know what changes the business environment requires as well as how best to implement those changes. Of course, no one likes change; and that includes the members of your team. Your leadership role however, dictates that you find the means to manage the resulting tensions successfully. Rightly motivated cause, clearly communicated vision, well-defined expectations, and the effective implementation of strategies and tactics are each important factors in your efforts.

As a leader, knowing why your business exists and what specific consumer need is being resolved is not only the foundation for success; it is, or should be, interwoven throughout every aspect of your business model. Since your company exists to provide a product or service that satisfies a legitimate consumer need, then *every* activity, no matter how seemingly mundane or complex, must contribute to that accomplishment.

Motivation

Speaking of change, I must address a bit of an aside that has presented itself in the course of my work to develop effective sales management training. The issue is motivation and how to effect change in people— change that is necessitated by the dynamics of business. Since a significant key to the success of a leader *is* his or her capacity to effect change, identifying the means to do so will provide a leader with an extremely helpful tool.

The question then is: "What makes people change?"

I have been taught that until someone experiences "enough discomfort" he or she will not change, and though I think that is true, I believe it is only half of the formula. People change because they believe that there is a good reason to do so, because they are *motivated* by the belief that their lives or the lives of those for whom they care will be improved, and though that improvement might be the reduction of discomfort, that improvement might also be the increase of comfort or some other desirable outcome. In other words, when a person values an outcome, when he or she considers a certain consequence worth the "cost," the actions required to obtain it will be undertaken. This leads to the understanding that how an individual defines rewards (and punishments for that matter) will determine how he or she is motivated, an understanding that is extremely valuable to a sales manager.

Motivation is defined as the cause or driving force behind the action that someone takes. I have seen, that as adults, motivation is self-imposed. By that, I mean that the actions I take are the end result, the effect as it were, of my values and my "causes." How I act is proof of what I believe. What I choose to do is a reflection of who I am as defined by my values. If I *believe* that a given discomfort is worth avoiding or that a certain reward is worth attaining, I will *act* in such a way as to achieve my goal—in other words, I am motivated.

The basis of motivation is the fact that we *have* to choose. In theory, if a person had everything he or she wanted, there would be no motivation. In reality; though we all have unlimited desires, our limited resources (time, money, energy, etc.) require us to choose where and how we will expend what resources we possess. Therefore, how or where we choose to spend our limited resources is the measurement of the value placed on the expenditure, an expression of what we believe to be important. When we can only afford one of the two options, the choice we make declares our priorities and values.

The disclosure of our priorities expresses itself quite dramatically in regards to our careers. Individuals' most valuable resource is their time; it is the one thing they can never have more of. They understand this innately. Since a person can only be in one place at a time, where a person spends his or her time is then a measure of the "cost" of that activity. Where a person spends the greatest amount of time has the greatest cost and this is true even if he or she *has* to rather than *wants* to spend time on that activity. For most people, the place they spend the greatest amount of their most valuable resource is at work. When they believe that that expenditure is a wise one, they will be motivated to continue making it and getting the most out of it. They will adopt what I refer to as an ownership attitude about their career. They are highly motivated.

If, on the other hand, they believe that they are wasting their resource, i.e., spending their time unwisely, they will be very reluctant to put forth any extra effort. This results in what I see as a debtor's attitude—they give what they have to, but no more—they are not at all motivated to put forth any extra effort.

A leader's role in this process then is two-fold. The first is to understand the values, drives, and priorities of those on his or her team. The second is to help his or her team members see the investment of their time in the workplace as a wise investment by declaring and demonstrating the importance of what they do for themselves and for the company.

The point is this: since motivations are the result of self-imposed beliefs *and* actions are the natural consequences of values—it is essential that I know what the people on my team consider to be important. If I, as a leader, am going to steer people toward more effective activities, I need to understand their values, clearly communicate the company's values and objectives, *and* help them to recognize the importance of their roles to the accomplishment of those objectives. If I do this well, I can help others be motivated to achieve the extraordinary.

In the final analysis, since all businesses exist to satisfy the legitimate needs of the customers and clients within the businesses' designated markets, doing so better than the competition *will* lead to growth in demand for the goods and/or services provided. If an employer, either by default or by directly employing conscientious leadership, experiences the benefits of consumer satisfaction—namely, loyalty and personal referrals—and the profitability toward which those benefits lead, that employer will thrive. Ideally (if only in recognition of what economists have known for generations—that a free market economy is driven by consumers), all businesses put the consumer first.

If, however, that ideal is not true where you work, so be it! You, as a leader, are still able to impart the importance of the end user to all those with whom you have influence. You can introduce and reinforce the right values in your domain, even if you are its lone citizen. That is what leaders do. They do what is right, not calling attention to themselves but focusing on those who will benefit from their actions.

And so it is: every purchase, every hiring, every report, every meeting, every activity at every level should be designed to strategically and effectively enable a business to achieve its objective. That objective, whether it is recognized or not, is always the same: to satisfy the needs of those consumers who are within the business's designated markets. Effective leaders understand these truths, communicate vision and passion to the team, and help them understand their importance to the achievement of success.

CHAPTER TWELVE
Single Focus

There is an ancient proverb that declares that servants cannot divide their service between two masters. The point is simple and poignant—we do not have the capacity to split our loyalties between two differing causes. And though the concept of servanthood is passé, the principles of loyalty and dedication still apply

To be effective, to accomplish exceptional results, there must be a single focus. Greatness requires dedication; dedication is the quality of being devoted or committed to something. The effort required to achieve superior results does not leave time or energy for distractions, let alone compromise.

Yet, businesses are often trying to do just that—strike a compromise between what clients want and profits. The question is: who is the master?

I opened the first chapter of this section describing the extraordinary characteristics of leaders and sharing my admiration of William Wallace for the leadership he provided the land of Scotland at a time when she faced almost certain conquest. What set Wallace apart then and influences is status as a hero still, was the singleness of focus with which he was dedicated to the freedom of his fellow Scots. Though he was himself a landowner, and therefore could have benefited from the "treaties" used by the English to gain a foothold in Scotland, he did not allow his loyalties to be split. William Wallace understood that ultimately there could only be one king, only one master. Any attempt to compromise would result in the denial of his convictions—and ultimately the betrayal of the people he loved.

Again, I recognize the risk I face of appearing to overstate the importance of Sales Management by using a role model such as William Wallace. However, history demonstrates that the principles of leadership are the same no matter the scope. If singleness of focus helped to enable Wallace and those he lead to accomplish great things for the people of Scotland, then it is also a principle that leaders in the business realm should consider as a means to help them achieve greatness. It is my assumption that no one who has read this far is looking for a way to be average, but for the means to be exceptional: being single focused *is* one such means.

* * *

What of those businesses and leaders who are trying to determine if they can make increasing profitability *and* satisfying the consumer their primary cause? For them the proverb applies: you cannot serve two masters. You will love the consumer or ignore him; you will cling to profitability or make it consequential to the fulfillment of your mission. Only one or the other can be your priority: at some point in time the two causes will oppose one another. There will come a situation when the pursuit of profitability will require abandoning the consumer's best interest. When that situation arises, your true master, your true priority, will become known.

* * *

If I, as a business owner or leader, decide to make profitability the center of my attention, my primary goal and objective, then my activities will be driven by efficiency, cost-savings, and personal fulfillment. I will view prospects, customers, and clients as the means to my end, as the source of my own success. Eventually, this mentality leads to my choosing that "master" over the consumer. As this mindset becomes apparent to the consumer, he or she will exercise the free-market opportunity to seek a business that *will* make satisfying his or her needs its priority. This will ultimately leave me with fewer and fewer consumers to satisfy. Sooner or later, my profit-driven model will fail because the only source of profits—the consumer—will not knowingly or willingly support it.

On the other hand, I can choose to focus on satisfying the wants and needs of consumers—to serve them. To "serve" means to furnish or supply with something needed or desired, to answer the needs of another. Based on that definition then, it could be said that the fundamental purpose of any business is to serve the consumer; businesses are here to satisfy the needs of customers and clients. And since clients and customers appreciate their wants and needs being satisfied they are happy to reward those businesses that do.

The undeniable dynamic is that by choosing to serve the needs of the consumer, by making them the "master" and the single focus of *all* business activity, your company earns the loyalty of those served. This loyalty will be revealed in two ways: repeat business *and* personal referrals from your loyal clients to those whose needs you will also be able to meet. It is no mere coincidence that every business that provides solutions to the consuming public has, as a part of its organizational structure, a "customer service" department. Satisfaction starts with the sale, but requires a service philosophy to be complete.

Interestingly, there is a paradox often experienced when a business makes serving the consumer its priority: what it was willing to set aside for the sake of making a priority of treating people respectfully (which, by the way is how you like to be treated when you are the consumer), it will re-gain as a natural by-product of putting the client's success first. In the long run, consumer satisfaction (cause) is the best way for a business to become and remain profitable (effect); it does not, however, work the other way.

* * *

The reality is that the consumer is in the driver's seat of all business transactions. Consumers constitute, directly or indirectly, nearly 95% of economic activity in the United States. Consumers (a category to which we all belong) want to have their needs satisfied; they (we) want to be treated with respect and will reward those providers of goods and services who treat them the way they *want* to be treated. Any approach that chooses profitability over consumer satisfaction, which chooses to serve self-interest over client-interest, will meet with failure; it is only a matter of time.

On the other hand, making the effective satisfaction of consumers the single focus of a business—making the consumer "master"—leads to the opportunity to satisfy more consumers' needs. Paradoxically, when a business puts customers first, makes their needs more important than its own, the business ultimately enjoys success on the customer satisfaction front *and* the profitability front.

To be sure, there will be challenges. There are likely to be competitors whose approach is self-centered, who seem to experience success, at least in the short-term. There will be times when being true to your convictions will stand, or at least appear to stand, in opposition to those who judge your effectiveness and who are not aware of the long-term track record that a consumer-driven model has for success. In the face of those challenges, leaders must choose their focus, and the choice is theirs alone: that *is* leadership.

But these challenges are nothing compared to the ones that success itself will bring. One need only look at the roots and foundations of many of the now stumbling corporate icons to find a story of a start-up business with clear vision and unwavering service gone awry. Somehow, these mighty corporations have left their first love, and been lured into the snare of a profit-driven model despite the undeniable lessons from their own history; history that declared that their business success was found in identifying and satisfying the needs of consumers better than the competition. These companies seem to have begun a nearly unstoppable descent into ruin by misunderstanding the very cause of their own historical successes. I say *nearly* unstoppable because I do believe that it is possible, through diligent application and unceasing reaffirmation, to re-insert and revitalize the consumer-driven principles that once made them great.

After twenty-five years of personal experience and observation, I know at what point it seems most justifiable to waver and compromise one's standards, whether they be personal or business in nature, is when standing confidently in them is most needed. I will also say that I have never once been sorry for having stood firm on a consumer-driven model. I can't say the same for the times I chose not to. In each case, a choice was made; a single "master" was served.

CHAPTER THIRTEEN
If Leading Were Easy . . .

When I was trained to be a bank teller more than two decades ago, I was never asked to handle counterfeit money; I was exposed only to real, legitimate currency. The theory was that by being absolutely familiar with the true I would intuitively recognize and reject the false, no matter how convincing the counterfeit was. It was my job to *know* the real, in every detail and characteristic. That done, anything that was not real would (and did) stand out.

Throughout this book I have followed that same methodology— describing true leadership and leaving a discourse of the counterfeit to others. As I use this chapter to reiterate the significant traits of leadership, I will again address only the aspects and characteristics of *real* leadership, the kind businesses value and upon which sales organizations depend. I believe that clear knowledge of the true will enable you to recognize and reject the false, should it ever be presented to you.

* * *

Leaders are those who willingly set the example for those who are looking to them for direction and guidance. Leaders are extremely valuable—that is to say that they are rare and useful. Their scarcity is the result of the heavy demands placed upon them; their usefulness is measured by the positive impact leaders have on those around them, their ability to bring out the best from their team, and to garner desired results.

Leaders are made, not born. They are made through commitment to the principles and practices that produce lasting, positive results. They are made through discipline and diligence; through consistently doing what ordinary people would never endeavor to endure.

It may be stating the obvious, but leadership is not easy. Leaders must *draw* the team toward the desired goal by example, blazing the trail of success, and never *drive* them from behind. A leader is an individual of influence, impact, and inspiration; someone who can move not only himself or herself, but others as well—a leverage point and a power center. And leverage is an amazing principle; properly used, leverage allows you to move with modest effort what brute force alone cannot budge. So it is with leadership. There is no need to demand and dictate. Instead, set a good example and treat others with respect; this will bring out the best in those being led.

But leadership is not easy. It requires dedication, commitment, focus, skill, patience, vision, consistency—and that's just for starters! Leaders cannot just possess these attributes; leaders must excel at them. There is a general tendency toward mediocrity that leaders must not only reject but also overcome. To be mediocre is, by definition, to be ordinary; to be a leader is to be extraordinary. At its root, the word "mediocre" refers to making it only halfway up the mountain. Leaders are not ordinary and cannot stop halfway up any mountain—if they do, they are not leaders.

This tendency toward mediocrity is not only present in society and business, but is also interwoven in the very fabric of creation. The third law of thermodynamics, or entropy, states that in a closed system, by the processes inherent within the existence of the system, order is replaced by disorder, usable energy by unusable. For the universe, that is a problem because all possible sources of energy are already included, and therefore chaos is inevitable (theology, of course, provides a solution to that dilemma but that would be another book). For business, the prospects are not as dire; there are always new sources of energy available for a business. Leaders are one such source and thus bring real value to an organization. True leaders are that outside influence, that new source of usable energy that will restore order and productivity to a business.

What is true and necessary for a business in general is even more vital to the sales organization. Sales people require a significant amount and a renewable source of energy and so are highly dependent on their leaders.

Excelling in anything is not easy. Excelling in leadership requires serious dedication and an ongoing willingness to reexamine the accepted norms. Leaders must fight the tendency within themselves to become satisfied with yesterday's victories, yesterday's excellence. Leaders bring new ideas, new solutions, and innovations to the process. Leaders change the inevitable deterioration by introducing a new, creative energy into the system. Corporate America is full of stories of leaders coming in and revitalizing a business, turning it back from the edge of failure and bringing it instead into a new age of success. It is what leaders do!

One of the greatest aspects of the free market economy of which we are a part is the possibility of ownership participation; the potential inherent in ownership leads to excellence. Leaders know that giving others the freedoms of ownership releases extraordinary efforts and produces unexpected results. Leaders do not hold to the oft-proclaimed motto "don't reinvent the wheel" because leaders understand that there is much to be said for and gained from the very process of invention. Leaders also know that though it doesn't make sense to put more into a venture than one can hope to get out of it, ownership extends the limits of what can be attained. These qualities make leaders valuable, which is to say, rare and desirable—to any business.

Risk and Reward

Not everyone is a leader primarily because not everyone *wants* to lead—the risks are great... but then, so are the rewards.

The nature of leadership requires a willingness to assume risk, including taking responsibility for the consequences of your actions. But leaders are not foolhardy; the risks being taken must be reasonable, meaning they must be known and examined. In the investment industry, it is an accepted axiom that there is no truly risk-free investment; risks come in too wide a variety for that to be possible. Designing an investment portfolio, then, cannot be about avoiding risk; it can only be about managing risks. And so it is with business: risk is inherent, but leaders can manage it.

To calculate whether a given risk is manageable for an investment client, I must know their objective, their experience, and their timeframe. The same applies to leadership: if a leader knows where the team is going, what the experiences have been in the past, and how long the team has to achieve the goal, he or she can evaluate the available methods and means and choose the most reasonable option—but never without risk.

Leaders must know the destination and identify the objective; leaders then seek the way to accomplish that destiny successfully. Leaders know that there are dangers along the way: some can be avoided, some must be faced and overcome, but any destiny worth pursuing will include risk.

While these risks tend toward uncertainty, the clarity of vision leaders possess brings stability to the team. The more clearly the objective is expressed, the better it is known and understood. The more concise the directives, the more at ease the team will be. Knowing, with certainty, the desired destination prevents the inevitable detours, roadblocks, and hazards from deterring the leader or the team from striving for the goal.

Along with clear vision of the objective, leaders must also have a clear understanding of where they and the team are today. A course cannot be set until leaders recognize the *destination* and the *starting point*. Leaders must be aware of the state of the team to assess the "you are here." Thus, leaders must stay involved. And since the state of the team changes, sometimes almost daily, leaders must make frequent assessments, which can only result from frequent involvement.

Being a leader is not easy, but the rewards for your efforts are exceptional. You have the opportunity and ability to make a difference in the lives of those who work for you and for whom you work. You can improve the welfare of those you lead and build a reputation of trustworthiness and excellence.

Have you ever experienced being treated with respect while in the market place? Can you remember how much better it felt to have a sales person focus on you and your needs instead of their own? If so, then you know the impact of sales leadership. What if every day each one of your team members made *that* kind of impact on each one of their customers? Think about the success your team would experience; your company, and yes, even you. Now that would be an exceptional reward!

Miscellany

Before I wrap things up, I need to address a couple of additional, basic leadership concepts.

The first comes in the form of a question: "aren't all leaders?"

There is a fairly popular position in training circles as well as in society as a whole that holds "we are all leaders." It is a position, as you already know, I do not happen to share. While within the confines of our responsibilities and accountabilities we all can and should demonstrate appropriate behavior (characteristics such as diligence, integrity, professionalism, and expertise) and in that sense we all can and should exhibit leadership qualities. I do not accept however, any definition of leadership that so mitigates its importance, value, and significance as to suggest, "we are all leaders." That is just plain silly. That is not to say that we don't all have the *potential* to be leaders, for we do—it is just that not everyone is willing to pay the price.

In real life (and we all know this to be true), there are those who lead and those who *choose* not to. Leadership is what it is: identifying and communicating goals and objectives, providing direction and guidance, and being an influence on others toward the accomplishment of those goals and objectives. Not everyone fits that description. To suggest that everyone does is an insult to those who have made the sacrifice to lead.

The second item has to do with the leader's attitude toward those whom he or she is leading.

The characteristics of leadership that make it valuable can also make it susceptible to being abused. However, true leaders exemplify appropriate behavior and so would never do a thing without making sure that it would bring value to the team. For example, leaders would not introduce change just for change's sake, but because it would improve the team's opportunity for success.

Leaders understand that "new" does not automatically equate to "improved:" change is not always healthy, and not all energy is positive.

Therefore, *leaders do not expect blind compliance.* Leaders must be willing to be proved and should never be threatened by that process. Those being led not only can but also absolutely should make sure they are being led in the right direction and to the right destination.

———◦———

Leadership is not easy, but it is extremely valuable.

Leaders can never succumb to the lure of the ordinary.

Leaders must innovate, but not just for the sake of change; instead, what new energy is inserted to the team is designed to better enable them to achieve the goal.

While all may possess the potential to lead, not all pay the price of leadership; though all should exemplify appropriate behavior, all cannot set the pace.

Leaders understand the inevitability of risk, never seeking to eliminate it, only to manage it effectively.

Leaders see. They see not only where the team needs to be, but where the team currently stands as well. Leaders know the state of the team because leaders are directly and frequently involved with each of the team members, and this involvement keeps their leadership pertinent, dynamic, and successful.

These are the characteristics and qualities of true leadership: knowing them is good; doing them is better; being them is best!

If leading were easy, anyone could do it, but not one would need it.

CHAPTER FOURTEEN

Beyond the Ordinary

I ended Section Two with the principle that though we all have the potential to lead, not everyone is willing to pay the price leadership requires. True leaders are extraordinary people; they have vision, passion, focus, and the ability to help others succeed. Being a leader is not easy—if it were, anyone could do it, but no one would need it. Therefore, your decision to take on the role and responsibilities of leadership is to be commended; your willingness to lead in the right way is exceptional.

Your impact on the lives of your team members is significant; their success, in part, depends on you, but because you are a leader, you are ready, willing, and able to take that responsibility on. You understand that you have to stay close to your team but that "hands-on" is not the same thing as overbearing. Whether you hired or inherited your team, you have taken the time to know their strengths and their weaknesses, and you respect them for both. You know the business objective, your priorities, and how to communicate them to the team. You have a clear definition of success, know what your team needs to achieve it, and have made sure that the requisite opportunity for that success has been provided.

You are fully aware that there will be times when you will have to revolt against the norm, and so will your team—it is the only way to provide consumers with the innovation they demand. You recognize that the sales persons are the most valuable resource your company has, for they match the company's solutions to the consumers' needs and make success possible.

You have started down the course to success, determined to stay true to it to the end, knowing what skills and aptitudes you need to get you and your team across the finish line. Because your vision is clear, you are able to see the obstacles that invariably crop up along the way: because you know the objective, you have made sure that you are equipped to remove those obstacles from the path.

You have embraced the truth that innovation is risky, but that its rewards make it worthwhile, and so you share ownership and encourage innovation, thereby bringing out the very best in your team.

Perfection is not an option, not in products, not in sales people, not even in yourself; but pursuing and providing the best *is* an option, and as a leader, it is your *only* option.

Just as your team needs mentoring, so will you. Find someone whom you admire, whose strengths offset your weaknesses, and whose achievements you want to emulate; let him or her mentor you and then make yourself available to mentor someone else. Encourage and participate in the dynamic flow of expertise. The rewards will be remarkable, because when you give the consuming public what they want (expertise), they are happy to reward you with their loyalty and help you achieve success.

As a leader you are not and never will be satisfied with normal or average; you desire the extraordinary and the exceptional. Stay true to what you know works: putting the client first—giving them what they want, equipping and enabling your team to be the best they can be, and always encouraging innovation—in yourself and in those you lead.

My hope for you is success—this guide is my way of helping make that possible.

Post Script

There were places in these pages where it was necessary for me to be agonizingly general. If not, I would risk making the mistake of trying to prescribe a specific solution without knowing your specific need. If you have questions about how to apply the principles and philosophies I have laid out or if you would benefit from further communication with my team or myself please feel free to email me at jlivesay@mac.com.

Thank you once again for the investment of your time and for allowing me the opportunity to influence your journey beyond the ordinary.

Godspeed!

www.ingramcontent.com/pod-product-compliance
Lightning Source LLC
Chambersburg PA
CBHW031840170526
45157CB00001B/373